D1712584

DAILY
Word Ladders

Grades 4–6

by Timothy V. Rasinski
Kent State University

New York • Toronto • London • Auckland • Sydney
Mexico City • New Delhi • Hong Kong • Buenos Aires

Teaching
Resources

To my own children—Mike, Emily, Mary, and Jenny—
Word Wizards in their own right.

A father couldn't ask for better kids.

Cover design by Maria Lilja

Interior design by Ellen Matlach for Boultinghouse & Boultinghouse, Inc.

Interior illustrations by Teresa Anderko

ISBN: 978-0-545-37488-0

Contents

Welcome to Word Ladders!

In this book you'll find 100 mini word-study lessons that are also kid-pleasing games! To complete each Word Ladder takes just ten minutes but actively involves each learner in analyzing the structure and meaning of words. To play, students begin with one word and then make a series of other words by changing or rearranging the letters in the word before. With regular use, Word Ladders can go a long way toward developing your students' decoding and vocabulary skills.

How do Word Ladders work?

Let's say our first Word Ladder begins with the word *walk*. The directions will tell students to change one letter in *walk* to make a word that means "to speak." The word students will make, of course, is *talk*. The next word will then ask students to make a change in *talk* to form another word—perhaps *chalk* or *tall*. At the top of the ladder, students will have a final word that is in some way related to the first word—for example, *run*. If students get stuck on a rung along the way, they can come back to it, because the words before and after will give them the clues they need to go on.

How do Word Ladders benefit students?

Word Ladders are great for building students' decoding, phonics, spelling, and vocabulary skills. When students add or rearrange letters to make a new word from one they have just made, they must examine sound-symbol relationships closely. This is just the kind of analysis that all children need to perform in order to learn how to decode and spell accurately. And when the puzzle adds a bit of meaning in the form of a definition (for example, "make a word that means *to say something*"), it helps extend students' understanding of words and concepts. All of these skills are key to students' success in learning to read and write. So even though Word Ladders will feel like a game, your students will be practicing essential literacy skills at the same time!

How do I teach a Word Ladder lesson?

Word Ladders are incredibly easy and quick to implement. Here are four simple steps:

1. Choose one of the 100 Word Ladders to try. (The last three pages are the hardest ladders in the book, so avoid starting with those.)

2. Make a copy of the Word Ladder for each student.

3. Choose whether you want to do the Word Ladder with the class as a whole, or have students work alone, in pairs, or in groups. When working with the whole class, use the CD to display the ladder on your interactive whiteboard (see "Using the CD" for more).

4. At each new word, students will see two clues: the kinds of changes they need to make to the previous word ("rearrange the letters" or "add two letters"), and a definition of or clue to the meaning of the new word. Sometimes this clue will be a cloze sentence in which the word fits the context but is left out for children to fill in. Move from word to word this way, up the whole Word Ladder.

Look for the **Bonus Boxes** with stars. These are particularly difficult words you may want to preteach.

That's the lesson in a nutshell! Once you're done, you may wish to extend the lesson by having students sort the words into various categories. This can help them deepen their understanding of word relationships. For instance, they could sort them into:

- Grammatical categories. (Which words are nouns? Verbs?)

- Word structure. (Which words have a long vowel and which don't? Which contain a consonant blend?)

- Word meaning. (Which words express what a person can do or feel? Which do not?)

Tips for Working With Word Ladders

To provide extra help, list all the answers for the ladder (that is, the words for each rung) on the board for students to choose from as they go through the puzzle. In addition:

- Add your own clues to give students extra help as they work through each rung of a ladder.

- If students are having difficulty with a particular word, you might simply say the word aloud and see if students can spell it correctly by making appropriate changes in the previous word.

- If students are stuck on a particular rung of the Word Ladder, tell them to skip it and come back to it later.

- Challenge students to come up with alternative definitions for the same words. Many words, like *lock, fall,* and *stock,* have multiple meanings.

Using the CD

The CD features the same Word Ladders that are in the book, ready to display on your interactive whiteboard. The Word Ladders on the CD were created using Promethean's ActivInspire software. To use, simply download the free Personal Edition of the software at http://www.prometheanplanet.com/en-us/support/software/activinspire/ and install into your computer. (You may need to register first before you can download the software. Registration is also free.)

Here are some tips for using the Word Ladders on the interactive whiteboard:

- Use the Page Browser to scan through the Word Ladders in the file. The ladders appear in the same order as they do in the book. To go to a desired page, simply tap on it on the browser.

- Invite students to use the Pen tool to write the answer to each clue on the write-on lines. To check if the answer is correct, drag down the Answer tab below the clue.

- To clear the page and hide the Answer tabs again, simply tap the reset button (two arrows forming a circle).

- Tap on the left or right arrows to move from page to page.

Name _____

Read the clues, then write the words.
Start at the bottom and climb to the top.

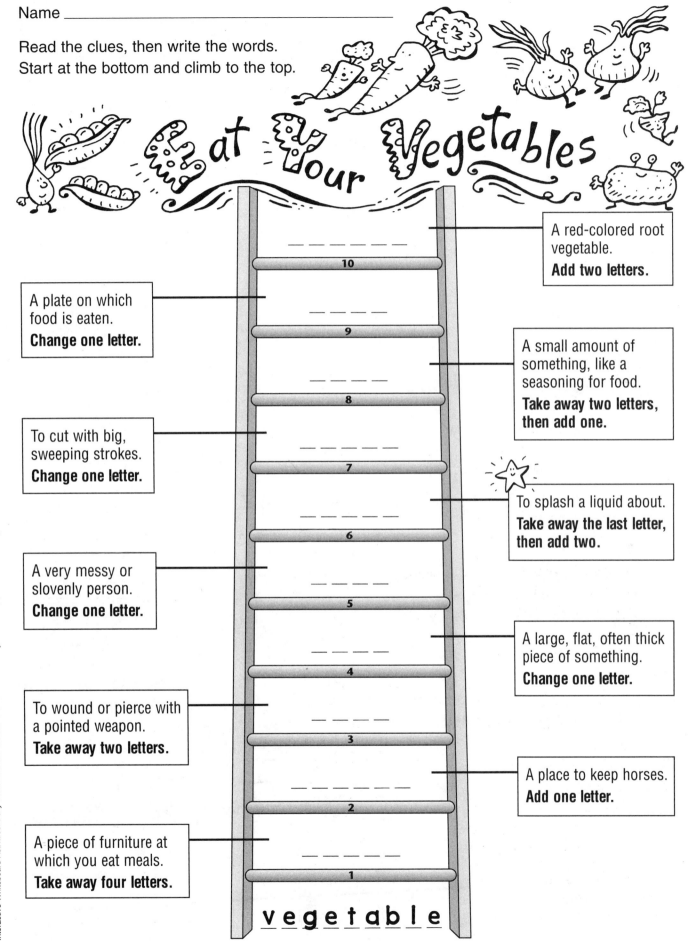

Eat Your Vegetables

A red-colored root vegetable.
Add two letters.

A plate on which food is eaten.
Change one letter.

A small amount of something, like a seasoning for food.
Take away two letters, then add one.

To cut with big, sweeping strokes.
Change one letter.

To splash a liquid about.
Take away the last letter, then add two.

A very messy or slovenly person.
Change one letter.

A large, flat, often thick piece of something.
Change one letter.

To wound or pierce with a pointed weapon.
Take away two letters.

A place to keep horses.
Add one letter.

A piece of furniture at which you eat meals.
Take away four letters.

10
9
8
7
6
5
4
3
2
1

v e g e t a b l e

Interactive Whiteboard Activities: Daily Word Ladders Grades 4–6 © 2012 Timothy V. Rasinski, Scholastic Teaching Resources

Name _____

Read the clues, then write the words.
Start at the bottom and climb to the top.

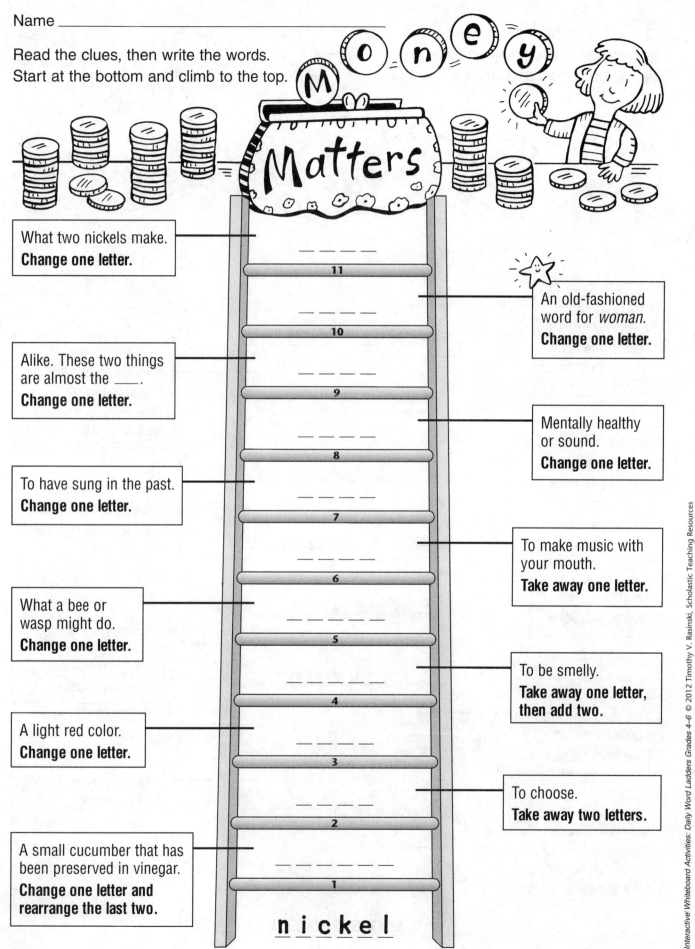

Money Matters

What two nickels make.
Change one letter.

‾ ‾ ‾ ‾
11

‾ ‾ ‾ ‾
10

An old-fashioned
word for *woman*.
Change one letter.

Alike. These two things
are almost the ___.
Change one letter.

‾ ‾ ‾ ‾
9

‾ ‾ ‾ ‾
8

Mentally healthy
or sound.
Change one letter.

To have sung in the past.
Change one letter.

‾ ‾ ‾ ‾
7

‾ ‾ ‾ ‾
6

To make music with
your mouth.
Take away one letter.

What a bee or
wasp might do.
Change one letter.

‾ ‾ ‾ ‾ ‾
5

‾ ‾ ‾ ‾ ‾
4

To be smelly.
**Take away one letter,
then add two.**

A light red color.
Change one letter.

‾ ‾ ‾ ‾
3

‾ ‾ ‾ ‾
2

To choose.
Take away two letters.

A small cucumber that has
been preserved in vinegar.
**Change one letter and
rearrange the last two.**

‾ ‾ ‾ ‾ ‾ ‾
1

n i c k e l

8

Interactive Whiteboard Activities: Daily Word Ladders Grades 4–6 © 2012 Timothy V. Rasinski, Scholastic Teaching Resources

Name _____

Read the clues, then write the words.
Start at the bottom and climb to the top.

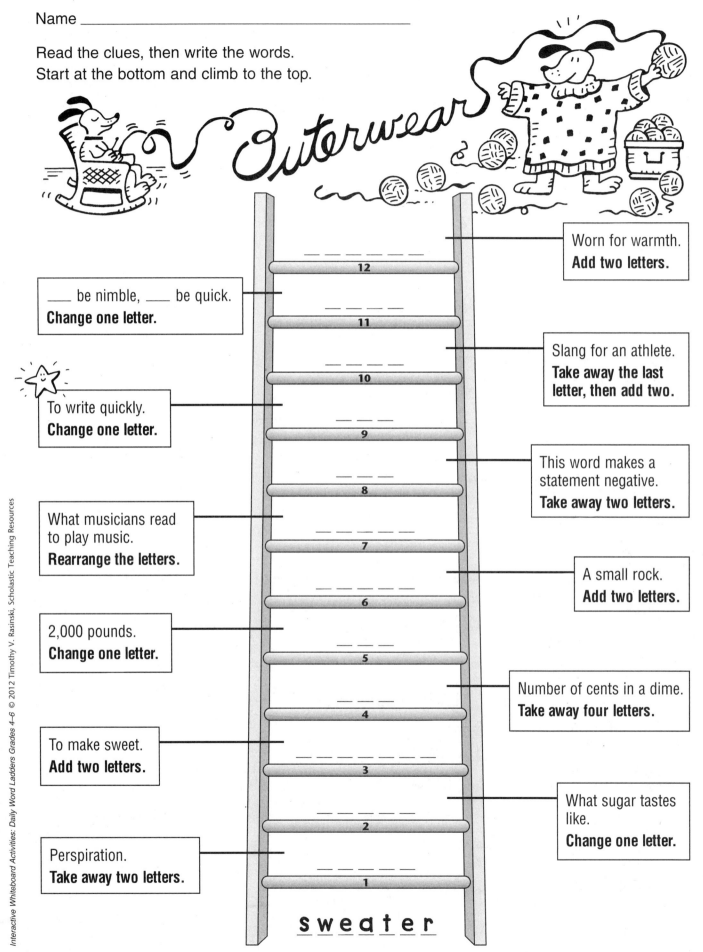

Outerwear

Worn for warmth.
Add two letters.

___ be nimble, ___ be quick.
Change one letter.

Slang for an athlete.
Take away the last letter, then add two.

To write quickly.
Change one letter.

This word makes a statement negative.
Take away two letters.

What musicians read to play music.
Rearrange the letters.

A small rock.
Add two letters.

2,000 pounds.
Change one letter.

Number of cents in a dime.
Take away four letters.

To make sweet.
Add two letters.

What sugar tastes like.
Change one letter.

Perspiration.
Take away two letters.

12
11
10
9
8
7
6
5
4
3
2
1

s w e a t e r

Interactive Whiteboard Activities: Daily Word Ladders Grades 4–6 © 2012 Timothy V. Rasinski, Scholastic Teaching Resources

Name _____

Read the clues, then write the words.
Start at the bottom and climb to the top.

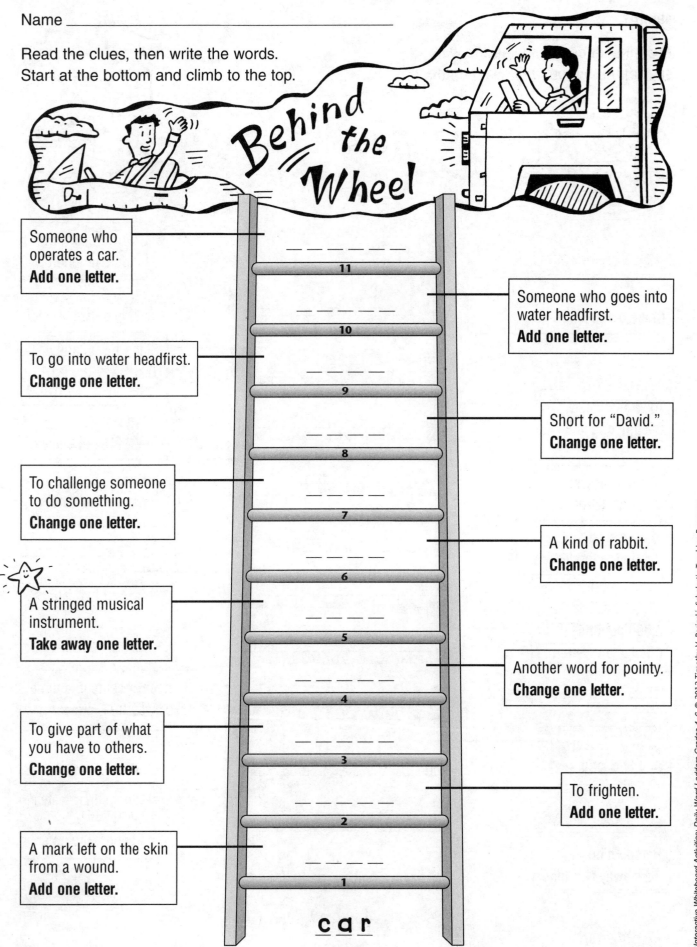

Behind the Wheel

Someone who operates a car.
Add one letter.

_ _ _ _ _ _ 11

Someone who goes into water headfirst.
Add one letter.

_ _ _ _ _ 10

To go into water headfirst.
Change one letter.

_ _ _ _ _ 9

Short for "David."
Change one letter.

_ _ _ _ 8

To challenge someone to do something.
Change one letter.

_ _ _ _ 7

A kind of rabbit.
Change one letter.

_ _ _ _ _ 6

A stringed musical instrument.
Take away one letter.

_ _ _ _ 5

Another word for pointy.
Change one letter.

_ _ _ _ _ 4

To give part of what you have to others.
Change one letter.

_ _ _ _ _ 3

To frighten.
Add one letter.

_ _ _ _ _ 2

A mark left on the skin from a wound.
Add one letter.

_ _ _ _ 1

c a r

Interactive Whiteboard Activities: Daily Word Ladders Grades 4–6 © 2012 Timothy V. Rasinski, Scholastic Teaching Resources

Name _____

Read the clues, then write the words.
Start at the bottom and climb to the top.

Give a Little

The opposite of give.
Take away one letter.

11 _ _ _ _ _

A pointed wooden stick to be driven into the ground.
Change one consonant.

10 _ _ _ _ _

A legless reptile.
Change one letter.

9 _ _ _ _ _

To vibrate.
Change one letter.

8 _ _ _ _ _

To cut hair with a razor.
Add one letter.

7 _ _ _ _ _

To possess something.
Change one letter.

6 _ _ _ _

Where bees live.
Change one letter.

5 _ _ _ _

To jump headfirst into water.
Take away one letter.

4 _ _ _ _

A person who dives.
Change one letter.

3 _ _ _ _ _

An organ in your body.
Add one letter.

2 _ _ _ _

To be alive.
Change one letter.

1 _ _ _ _

g i v e

Name _____

Read the clues, then write the words.
Start at the bottom and climb to the top.

Things That Go Bump in the Night

A nocturnal animal that flies.
Change one letter.

A wager that something will happen.
Change one letter.

What fishermen use.
Rearrange letters.

5 + 5 = ___.
Change one letter.

2,000 pounds.
Take away one letter.

Musical sound.
Change one letter.

A prong on a fork.
Change one letter.

Synonym for *good*.
Change one letter.

When something is set ablaze it makes this.
Change one letter.

Used on a car for a wheel.
Take away two letters.

To stop working, usually at a certain age.
Change the first three letters.

When a ticket or license can't be used anymore, it has ___d.
Take away the first three letters, then add two.

12 _ _ _ _
11 _ _ _ _
10 _ _ _
9   _ _ _
8   _ _ _
7   _ _ _ _ _
6   _ _ _ _
5   _ _ _ _
4   _ _ _ _
3   _ _ _ _
2   _ _ _ _ _ _
1   _ _ _ _ _ _

v a m p i r e

Interactive Whiteboard Activities: Daily Word Ladders Grades 4–6 © 2012 Timothy V. Rasinski, Scholastic Teaching Resources

Name _____

Read the clues, then write the words.
Start at the bottom and climb to the top.

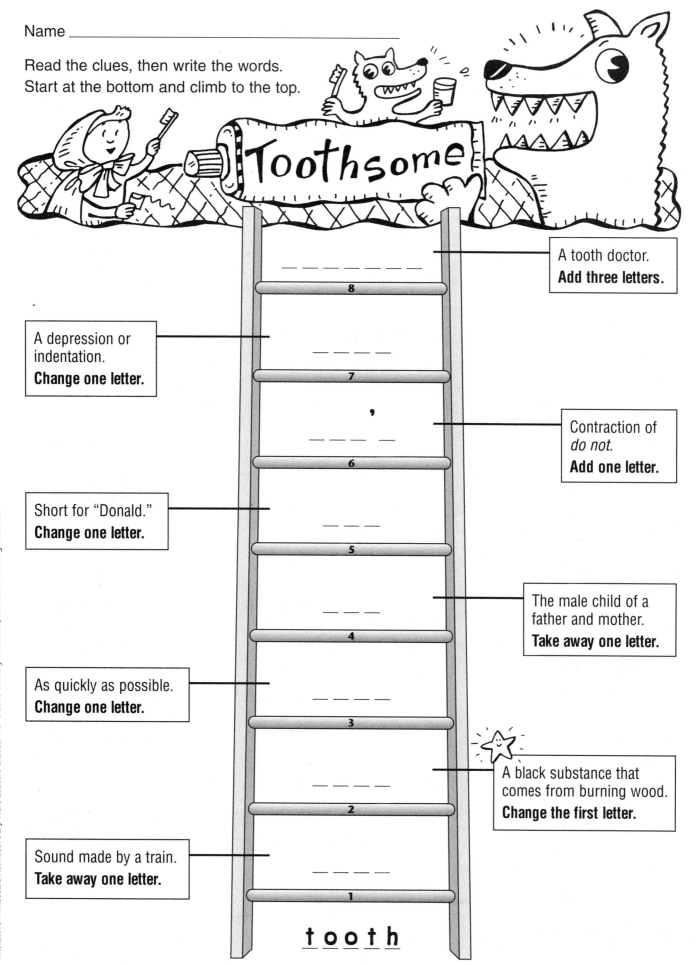

Toothsome

A tooth doctor.
Add three letters.

_ _ _ _ _ _ _ _ 8

A depression or
indentation.
Change one letter.

_ _ _ _ 7

Contraction of
do not.
Add one letter.

_ _ ' _ _ 6

Short for "Donald."
Change one letter.

_ _ _ 5

The male child of a
father and mother.
Take away one letter.

_ _ _ 4

As quickly as possible.
Change one letter.

_ _ _ _ 3

A black substance that
comes from burning wood.
Change the first letter.

_ _ _ _ 2

Sound made by a train.
Take away one letter.

_ _ _ _ _ 1

t o o t h

Name _____

Read the clues, then write the words.
Start at the bottom and climb to the top.

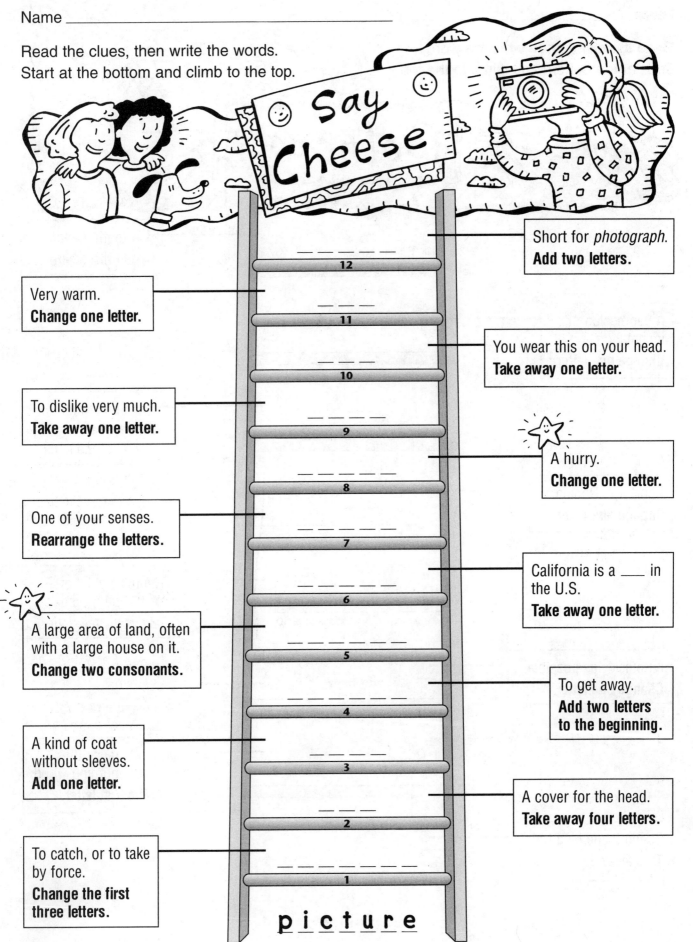

Say Cheese

Short for *photograph*.
Add two letters.

12 _ _ _ _ _

Very warm.
Change one letter.

11 _ _ _

You wear this on your head.
Take away one letter.

10 _ _ _ _

To dislike very much.
Take away one letter.

9 _ _ _ _ _

A hurry.
Change one letter.

8 _ _ _ _ _

One of your senses.
Rearrange the letters.

7 _ _ _ _ _

California is a ___ in the U.S.
Take away one letter.

6 _ _ _ _ _

A large area of land, often with a large house on it.
Change two consonants.

5 _ _ _ _ _ _

To get away.
Add two letters to the beginning.

4 _ _ _ _ _ _

A kind of coat without sleeves.
Add one letter.

3 _ _ _ _ _

A cover for the head.
Take away four letters.

2 _ _ _ _

To catch, or to take by force.
Change the first three letters.

1 _ _ _ _ _ _ _

p i c t u r e

14

Interactive Whiteboard Activities: Daily Word Ladders Grades 4–6 © 2012 Timothy V. Rasinski, Scholastic Teaching Resources

Name _____

Read the clues, then write the words.
Start at the bottom and climb to the top.

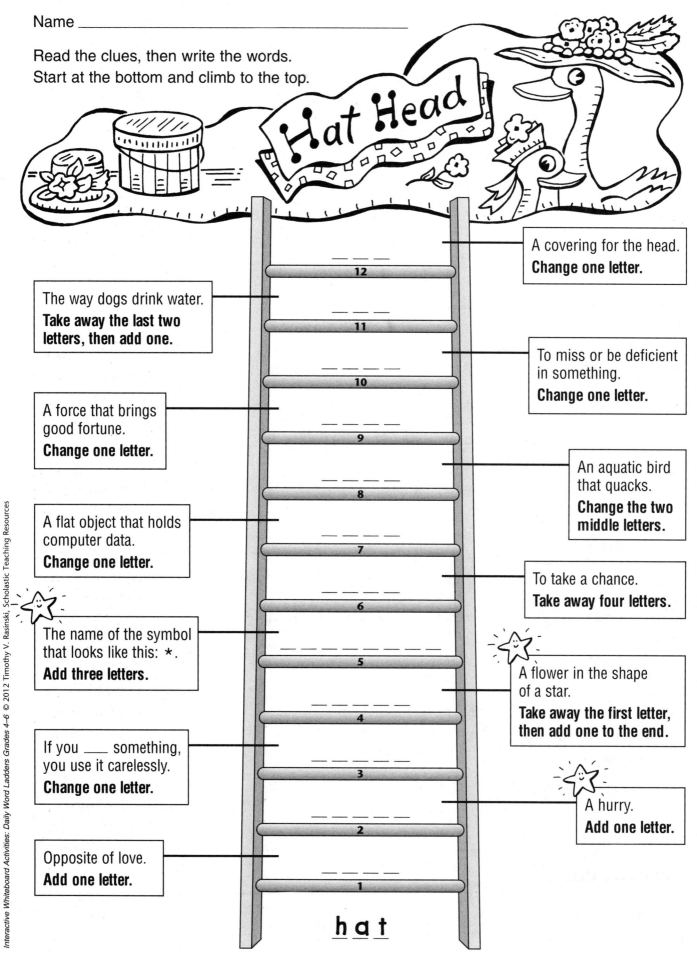

Hat Head

A covering for the head.
Change one letter.

The way dogs drink water.
Take away the last two letters, then add one.

To miss or be deficient in something.
Change one letter.

A force that brings good fortune.
Change one letter.

An aquatic bird that quacks.
Change the two middle letters.

A flat object that holds computer data.
Change one letter.

To take a chance.
Take away four letters.

The name of the symbol that looks like this: ✳.
Add three letters.

A flower in the shape of a star.
Take away the first letter, then add one to the end.

If you ___ something, you use it carelessly.
Change one letter.

A hurry.
Add one letter.

Opposite of love.
Add one letter.

12

11

10

9

8

7

6

5

4

3

2

1

h a t

Interactive Whiteboard Activities: Daily Word Ladders Grades 4–6 © 2012 Timothy V. Rasinski, Scholastic Teaching Resources

Name _____

Read the clues, then write the words.
Start at the bottom and climb to the top.

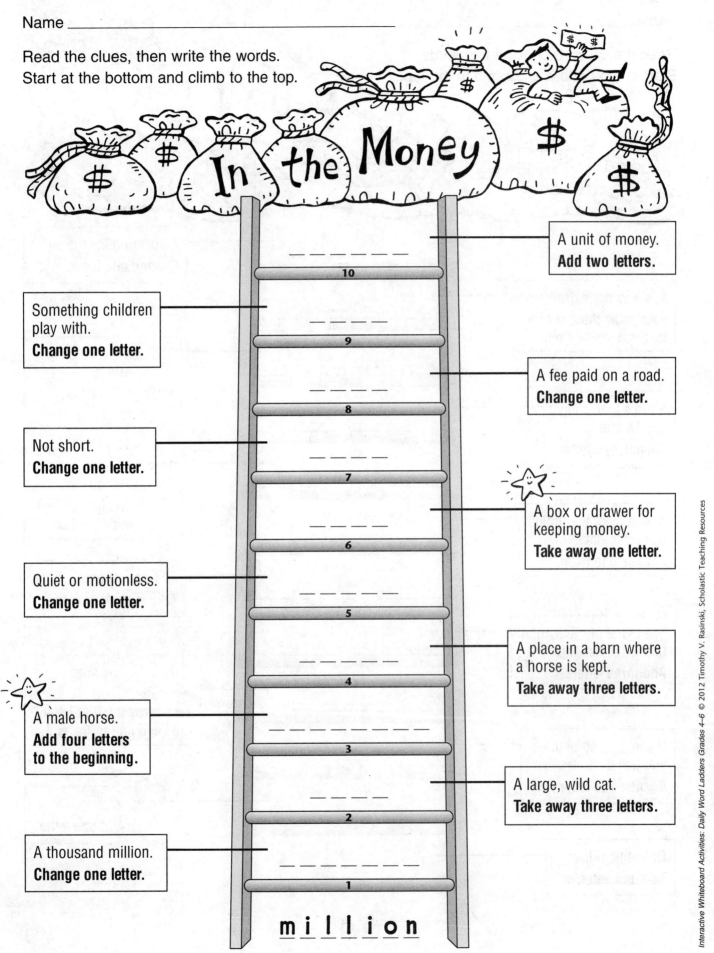

In the Money

A unit of money.
Add two letters.

Something children
play with.
Change one letter.

A fee paid on a road.
Change one letter.

Not short.
Change one letter.

A box or drawer for
keeping money.
Take away one letter.

Quiet or motionless.
Change one letter.

A place in a barn where
a horse is kept.
Take away three letters.

A male horse.
**Add four letters
to the beginning.**

A large, wild cat.
Take away three letters.

A thousand million.
Change one letter.

10

9

8

7

6

5

4

3

2

1

m i l l i o n

Interactive Whiteboard Activities: Daily Word Ladders Grades 4–6 © 2012 Timothy V. Rasinski, Scholastic Teaching Resources

Name _____

Read the clues, then write the words.
Start at the bottom and climb to the top.

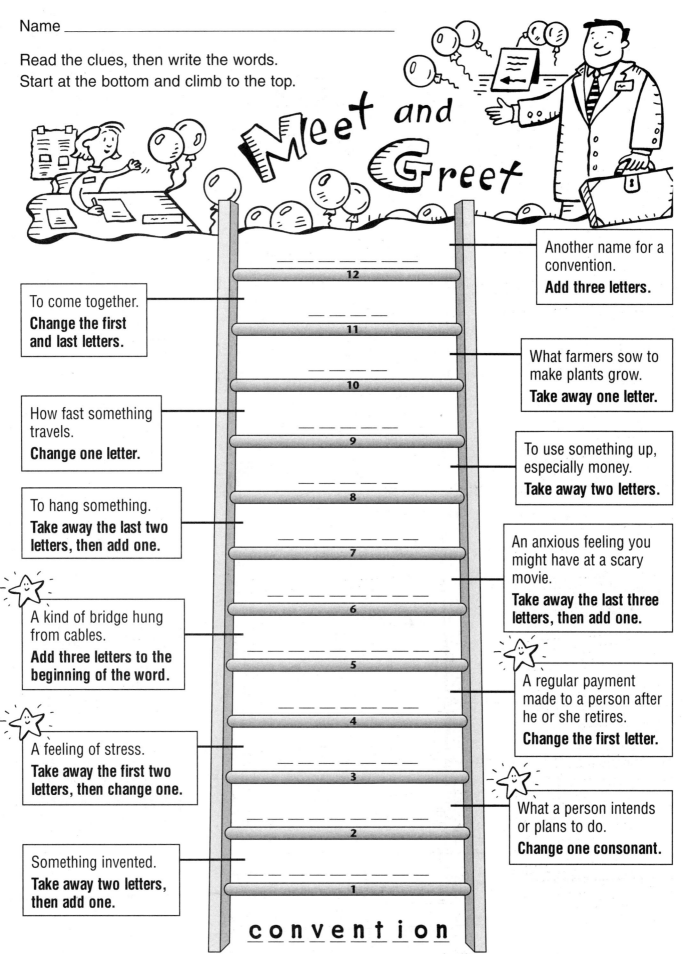

Meet and Greet

Another name for a convention.
Add three letters.

To come together.
Change the first and last letters.

What farmers sow to make plants grow.
Take away one letter.

How fast something travels.
Change one letter.

To use something up, especially money.
Take away two letters.

To hang something.
Take away the last two letters, then add one.

An anxious feeling you might have at a scary movie.
Take away the last three letters, then add one.

A kind of bridge hung from cables.
Add three letters to the beginning of the word.

A regular payment made to a person after he or she retires.
Change the first letter.

A feeling of stress.
Take away the first two letters, then change one.

What a person intends or plans to do.
Change one consonant.

Something invented.
Take away two letters, then add one.

12
11
10
9
8
7
6
5
4
3
2
1

c o n v e n t i o n

Interactive Whiteboard Activities: Daily Word Ladders Grades 4–6 © 2012 Timothy V. Rasinski, Scholastic Teaching Resources

Name _____

Read the clues, then write the words.
Start at the bottom and climb to the top.

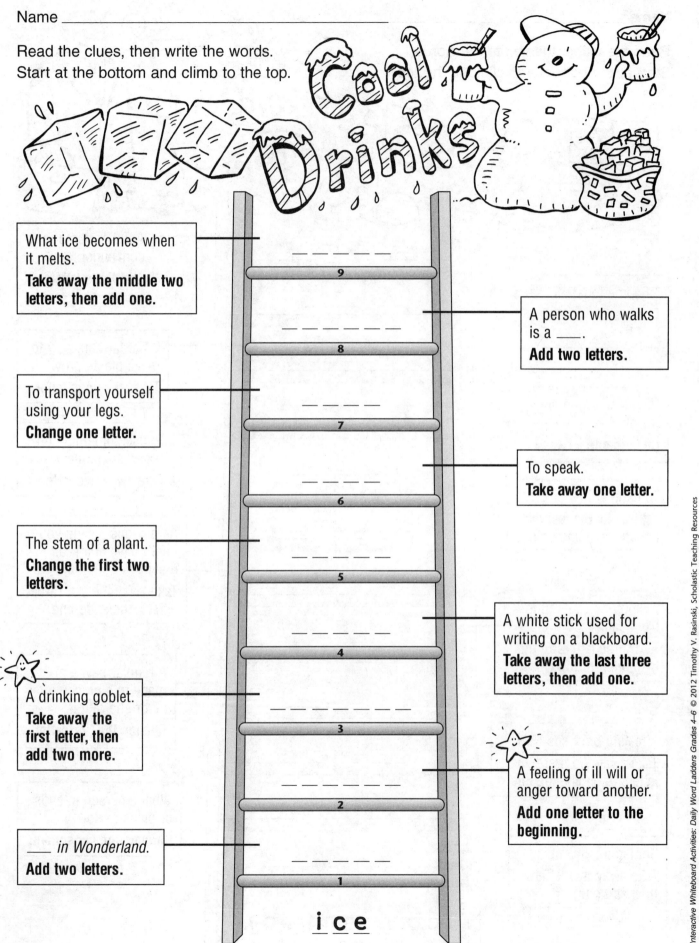

Cool Drinks

What ice becomes when it melts.
Take away the middle two letters, then add one.

9 _ _ _ _ _

A person who walks is a ___.
Add two letters.

8 _ _ _ _ _ _

To transport yourself using your legs.
Change one letter.

7 _ _ _ _ _

To speak.
Take away one letter.

6 _ _ _ _ _

The stem of a plant.
Change the first two letters.

5 _ _ _ _ _

A white stick used for writing on a blackboard.
Take away the last three letters, then add one.

4 _ _ _ _ _

A drinking goblet.
Take away the first letter, then add two more.

3 _ _ _ _ _ _

A feeling of ill will or anger toward another.
Add one letter to the beginning.

2 _ _ _ _ _ _

___ in Wonderland.
Add two letters.

1 _ _ _ _ _

i c e

18

Interactive Whiteboard Activities: Daily Word Ladders Grades 4–6 © 2012 Timothy V. Rasinski, Scholastic Teaching Resources

Name _____

Read the clues, then write the words.
Start at the bottom and climb to the top.

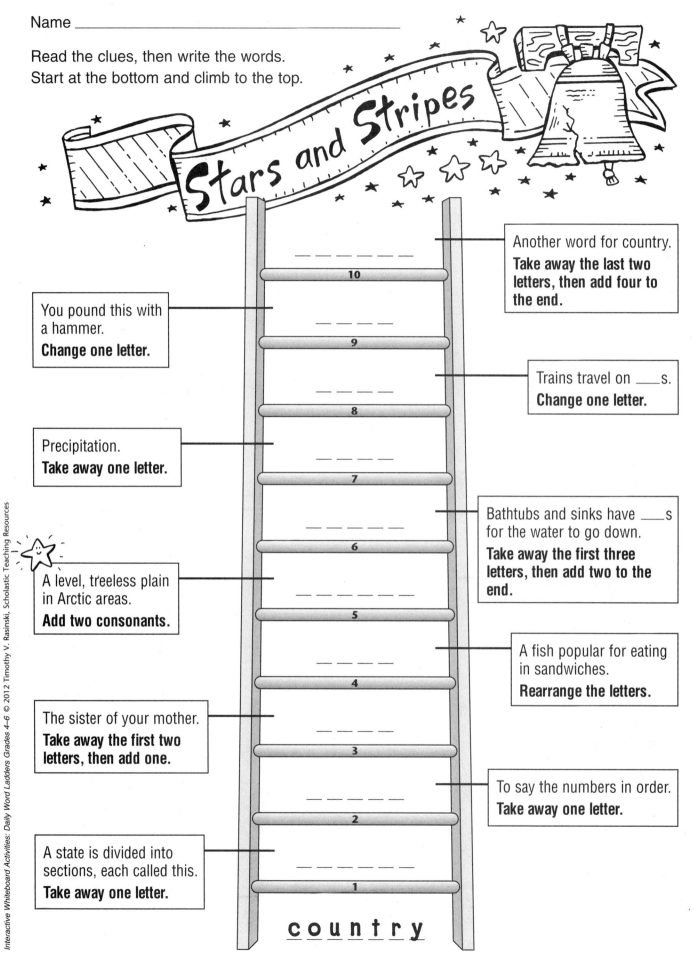

Stars and Stripes

Another word for country.
Take away the last two letters, then add four to the end.

You pound this with a hammer.
Change one letter.

Trains travel on ___s.
Change one letter.

Precipitation.
Take away one letter.

Bathtubs and sinks have ___s for the water to go down.
Take away the first three letters, then add two to the end.

A level, treeless plain in Arctic areas.
Add two consonants.

A fish popular for eating in sandwiches.
Rearrange the letters.

The sister of your mother.
Take away the first two letters, then add one.

To say the numbers in order.
Take away one letter.

A state is divided into sections, each called this.
Take away one letter.

10
9
8
7
6
5
4
3
2
1

c o u n t r y

Interactive Whiteboard Activities: Daily Word Ladders Grades 4–6 © 2012 Timothy V. Rasinski, Scholastic Teaching Resources

Name _____

Read the clues, then write the words.
Start at the bottom and climb to the top.

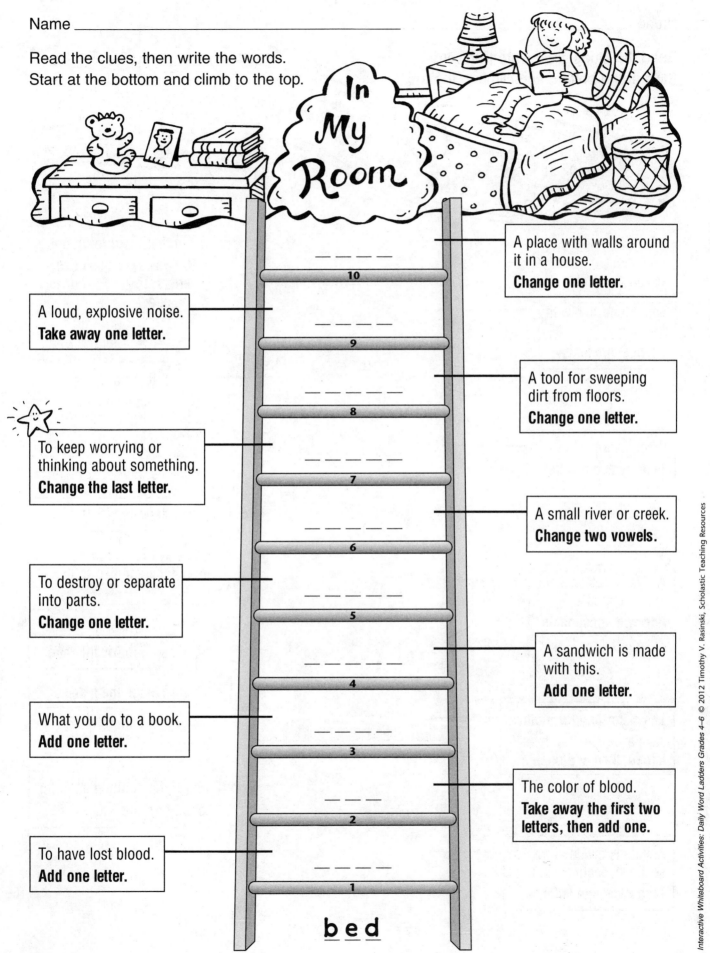

In My Room

A place with walls around it in a house.
Change one letter.

10 _ _ _ _ _

A loud, explosive noise.
Take away one letter.

9 _ _ _ _ _

A tool for sweeping dirt from floors.
Change one letter.

8 _ _ _ _ _

To keep worrying or thinking about something.
Change the last letter.

7 _ _ _ _ _

A small river or creek.
Change two vowels.

6 _ _ _ _ _

To destroy or separate into parts.
Change one letter.

5 _ _ _ _ _

A sandwich is made with this.
Add one letter.

4 _ _ _ _

What you do to a book.
Add one letter.

3 _ _ _ _

The color of blood.
Take away the first two letters, then add one.

2 _ _ _

To have lost blood.
Add one letter.

1 _ _ _ _

b e d

Interactive Whiteboard Activities: Daily Word Ladders Grades 4–6 © 2012 Timothy V. Rasinski, Scholastic Teaching Resources

Name _____

Read the clues, then write the words.
Start at the bottom and climb to the top.

Sleepytime

Something that goes
with a pillow.
Add two letters.

_ _ _ _ _ _ _
9

Fill in the ___.
Add one letter.

_ _ _ _ _
8

A place to put money.
Change one letter.

_ _ _ _ _
7

A container for holding
liquid or gas.
Change one letter.

_ _ _ _
6

To speak.
Change one consonant.

_ _ _ _
5

Not short.
Change one letter.

_ _ _ _
4

Another word for autumn.
Change one letter.

_ _ _ _
3

When you put water in a
glass, you ___ it up.
Change one letter.

_ _ _ _
2

Many medicines come
in this form.
Take away two letters.

_ _ _ _
1

p i l l o w

Name _____

Read the clues, then write the words.
Start at the bottom and climb to the top.

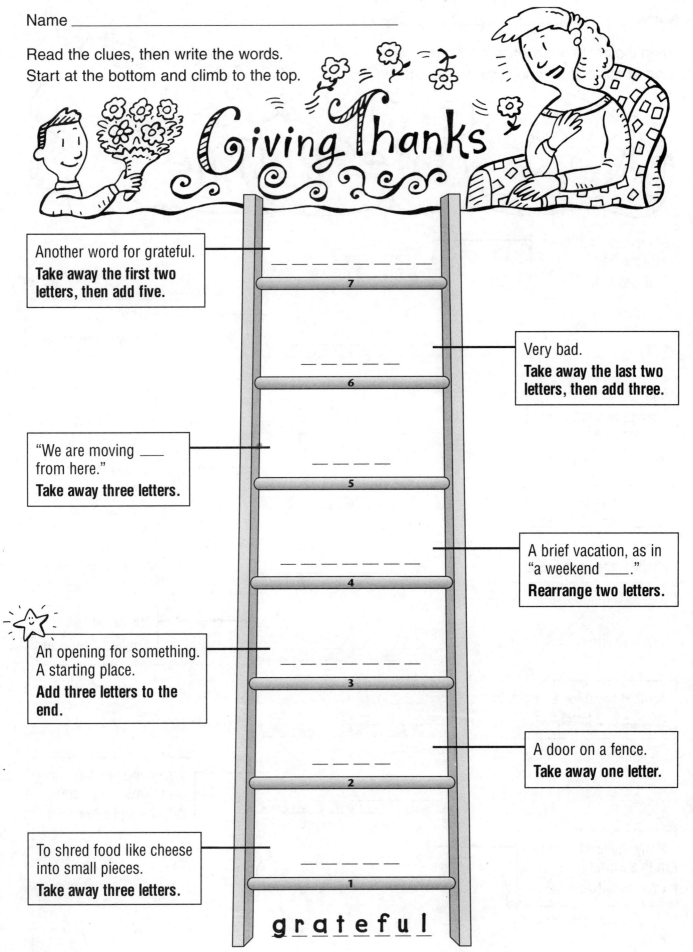

Another word for grateful.
Take away the first two letters, then add five.

Very bad.
Take away the last two letters, then add three.

"We are moving ___ from here."
Take away three letters.

A brief vacation, as in "a weekend ___."
Rearrange two letters.

An opening for something. A starting place.
Add three letters to the end.

A door on a fence.
Take away one letter.

To shred food like cheese into small pieces.
Take away three letters.

g r a t e f u l

Interactive Whiteboard Activities: Daily Word Ladders Grades 4–6 © 2012 Timothy V. Rasinski, Scholastic Teaching Resources

Name _____

Read the clues, then write the words.
Start at the bottom and climb to the top.

Express Mail

What you do to mail.
Change one letter.
— — — — 11

Grainy substance found on beaches.
Add one letter.
— — — — 10

Unhappy.
Change one letter.
— — — 9

Short for "Samuel."
Take away one letter.
— — — 8

To shut hard.
Change one letter.
— — — — 7

Thin.
Take away one letter.
— — — — 6

A gooey substance you might call *gross*.
Add one letter.
— — — — — 5

A citrus fruit.
Change one letter.
— — — — 4

Something you sometimes have to stand in while you wait.
Change one letter.
— — — — 3

To be alive.
Take away one letter.
— — — — 2

An organ in the body.
Take away two letters.
— — — — — 1

d e l i v e r

Interactive Whiteboard Activities: Daily Word Ladders Grades 4–6 © 2012 Timothy V. Rasinski, Scholastic Teaching Resources

Name _____

Read the clues, then write the words.
Start at the bottom and climb to the top.

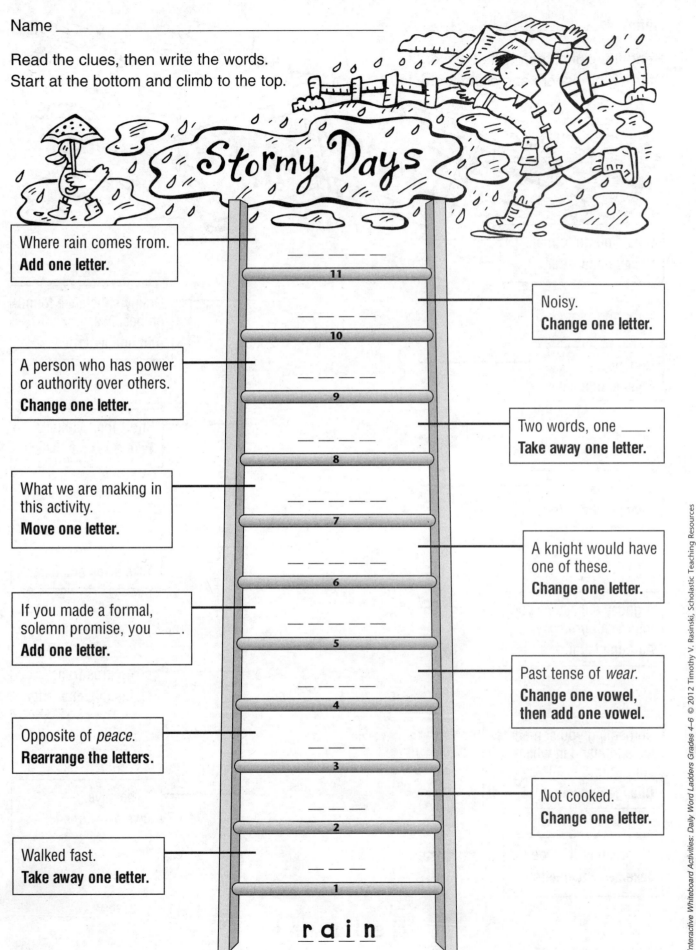

Stormy Days

Where rain comes from.
Add one letter.

11 _ _ _ _ _ _

Noisy.
Change one letter.

10 _ _ _ _

A person who has power
or authority over others.
Change one letter.

9 _ _ _ _

Two words, one ___.
Take away one letter.

8 _ _ _ _ _

What we are making in
this activity.
Move one letter.

7 _ _ _ _ _ _

A knight would have
one of these.
Change one letter.

6 _ _ _ _ _

If you made a formal,
solemn promise, you ___.
Add one letter.

5 _ _ _ _ _ _

Past tense of *wear*.
**Change one vowel,
then add one vowel.**

4 _ _ _ _

Opposite of *peace*.
Rearrange the letters.

3 _ _ _

Not cooked.
Change one letter.

2 _ _ _

Walked fast.
Take away one letter.

1 _ _ _

r a i n

Interactive Whiteboard Activities: *Daily Word Ladders Grades 4–6* © 2012 Timothy V. Rasinski, Scholastic Teaching Resources

Name _____

Read the clues, then write the words.
Start at the bottom and climb to the top.

Official Officers

Highest rank in the military.
Take away two letters.

8 _ _ _ _ _ _ _ _

Usually. "I ___ like sweets but don't want any today."
Take away the last four letters, then add three.

7 _ _ _ _ _ _ _ _ _

A group of people born and living at the same time.
Take away the last letter, then add three.

6 _ _ _ _ _ _ _ _ _

To produce or make electricity is to ___ it.
Add three letters after the _g_.

5 _ _ _ _ _ _ _ _ _

What you do to cheese to make it into small pieces.
Add one letter.

4 _ _ _ _ _ _

To judge or grade others or things.
Take away one letter.

3 _ _ _ _ _

Very angry.
Take away one letter.

2 _ _ _ _ _ _

Someone who steals from others on the high seas.
Take away one letter, then rearrange the second and third letters.

1 _ _ _ _ _ _ _

p r i v a t e

Interactive Whiteboard Activities: Daily Word Ladders Grades 4–6 © 2012 Timothy V. Rasinski, Scholastic Teaching Resources

Name _____

Read the clues, then write the words.
Start at the bottom and climb to the top.

Bucket Brigade

12 _ _ _ _

Another name for
a bucket.
**Change the last two
letters.**

To put clothes in a
suitcase.
Change one letter.

11 _ _ _ _

10 _ _ _ _

What you do to ripe
fruit on the tree or vine.
Change one letter.

Short for "Mickey."
Change one letter.

9 _ _ _ _

8 _ _ _ _

To ridicule another
person.
Change one letter.

Where boats are parked.
**Take away three letters,
then add one.**

7 _ _ _ _

6 _ _ _ _ _ _

A person who works to
heal the sick.
**Take away three letters,
then change one.**

A person who leads or
guides an orchestra or train.
Add two letters to the end.

5 _ _ _ _ _ _ _ _ _

4 _ _ _ _ _ _ _

To lead or guide an
orchestra or train.
**Add three letters
to the beginning.**

A kind of heavy tape.
Change the last letter.

3 _ _ _ _

2 _ _ _ _

An aquatic bird
that quacks.
Change one letter.

Another word for a dollar.
Take away two letters.

1 _ _ _ _

b u c k e t

26

Interactive Whiteboard Activities: Daily Word Ladders Grades 4–6 © 2012 Timothy V. Rasinski, Scholastic Teaching Resources

Name _____

Read the clues, then write the words.
Start at the bottom and climb to the top.

Sweet Things

The flavor of caramel.
Change one letter.

_ _ _ _ _
9

Perspiration.
Add one letter.

_ _ _ _ _
8

A place where one can sit.
Change one letter.

_ _ _ _
7

The place where two pieces
of cloth are sewn together.
Rearrange the letters.

_ _ _ _
6

Like something else
in all ways.
Change one letter.

_ _ _ _
5

Mentally sound or healthy.
Change one letter.

_ _ _ _
4

A long stick to help
with walking.
Change one letter.

_ _ _ _
3

To have come.
Take away one letter.

_ _ _ _
2

A desert animal.
Take away two letters.

_ _ _ _ _
1

c a r a m e l

Name _____

Read the clues, then write the words.
Start at the bottom and climb to the top.

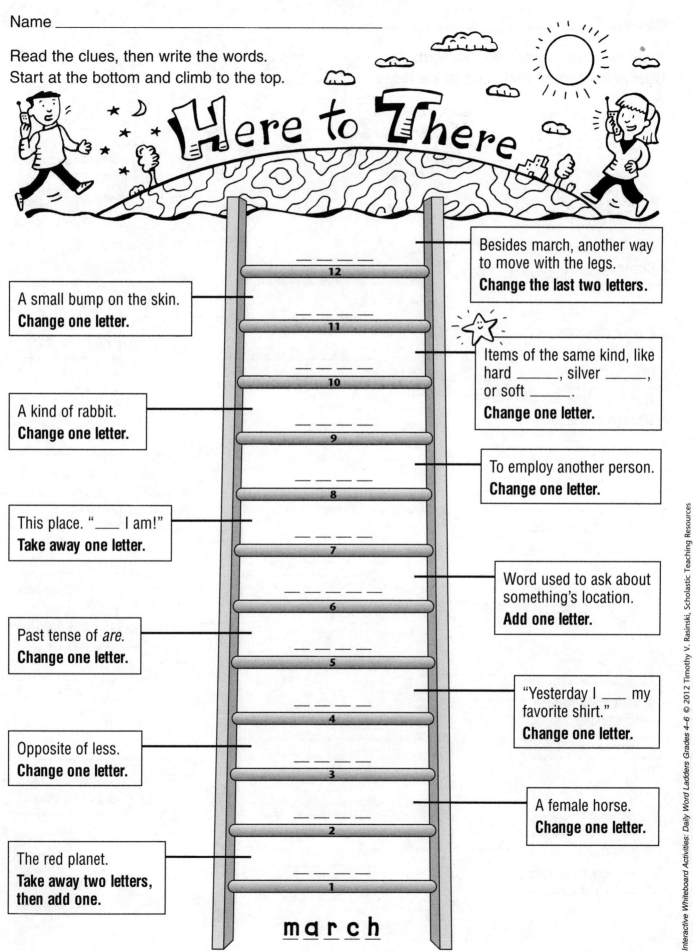

Here to There

Besides march, another way to move with the legs.
Change the last two letters.

A small bump on the skin.
Change one letter.

Items of the same kind, like hard _____, silver _____, or soft _____.
Change one letter.

A kind of rabbit.
Change one letter.

To employ another person.
Change one letter.

This place. "___ I am!"
Take away one letter.

Word used to ask about something's location.
Add one letter.

Past tense of *are*.
Change one letter.

"Yesterday I ___ my favorite shirt."
Change one letter.

Opposite of less.
Change one letter.

A female horse.
Change one letter.

The red planet.
Take away two letters, then add one.

12 _ _ _ _
11 _ _ _ _
10 _ _ _ _
9 _ _ _ _
8 _ _ _ _
7 _ _ _ _
6 _ _ _ _ _ _
5 _ _ _ _
4 _ _ _ _
3 _ _ _ _
2 _ _ _ _
1 _ _ _ _

m a r c h

Interactive Whiteboard Activities: Daily Word Ladders Grades 4–6 © 2012 Timothy V. Rasinski, Scholastic Teaching Resources

Name _____

Read the clues, then write the words.
Start at the bottom and climb to the top.

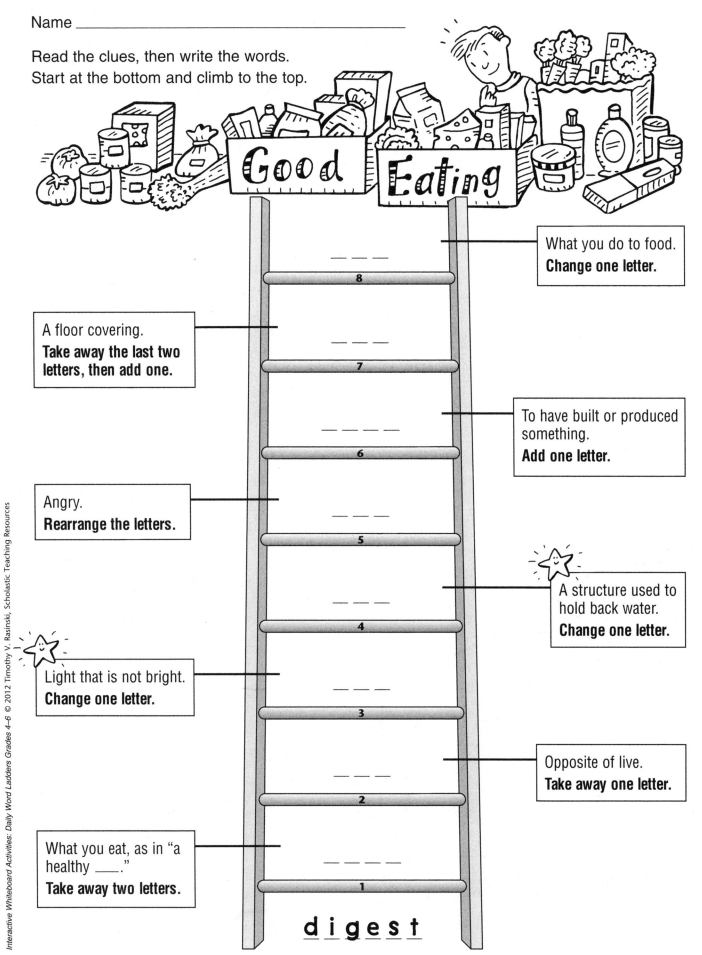

Good Eating

8 _ _ _ _

What you do to food.
Change one letter.

7 _ _ _

A floor covering.
Take away the last two letters, then add one.

6 _ _ _ _ _

To have built or produced something.
Add one letter.

5 _ _ _ _

Angry.
Rearrange the letters.

4 _ _ _

A structure used to hold back water.
Change one letter.

3 _ _ _

Light that is not bright.
Change one letter.

2 _ _ _ _

Opposite of live.
Take away one letter.

1 _ _ _ _ _

What you eat, as in "a healthy ___."
Take away two letters.

d i g e s t

Name _____

Read the clues, then write the words.
Start at the bottom and climb to the top.

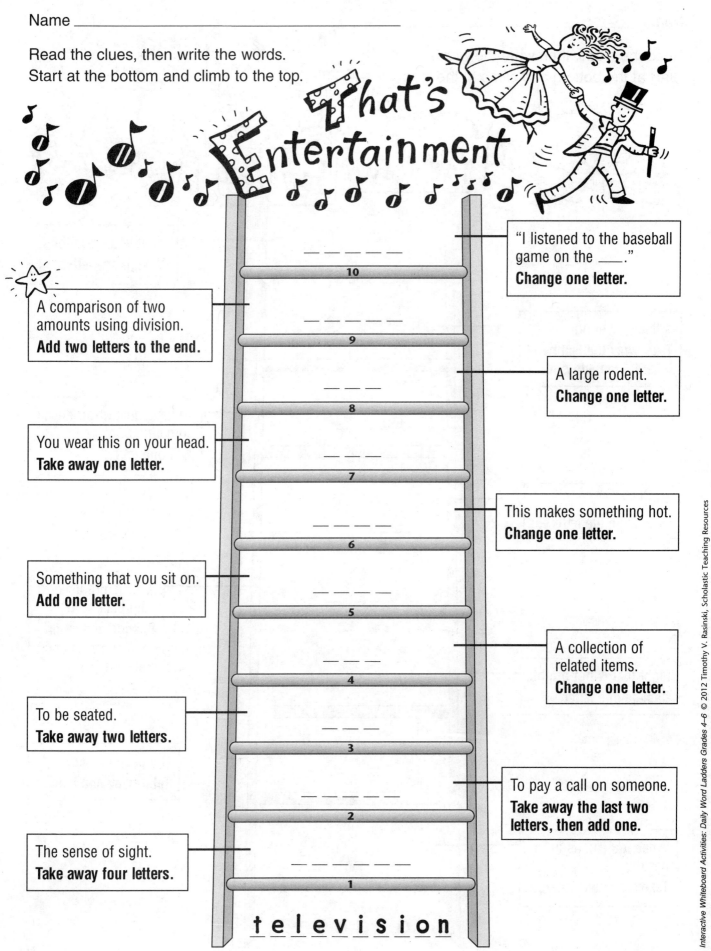

That's Entertainment

"I listened to the baseball game on the ___."
Change one letter.

A comparison of two amounts using division.
Add two letters to the end.

10 _ _ _ _ _ _

9 _ _ _ _ _

A large rodent.
Change one letter.

8 _ _ _

You wear this on your head.
Take away one letter.

7 _ _ _ _

This makes something hot.
Change one letter.

6 _ _ _ _ _

Something that you sit on.
Add one letter.

5 _ _ _ _

A collection of related items.
Change one letter.

4 _ _ _

To be seated.
Take away two letters.

3 _ _ _

To pay a call on someone.
Take away the last two letters, then add one.

2 _ _ _ _ _

The sense of sight.
Take away four letters.

1 _ _ _ _ _ _ _

t e l e v i s i o n

Interactive Whiteboard Activities: Daily Word Ladders Grades 4–6 © 2012 Timothy V. Rasinski, Scholastic Teaching Resources

Name _____

Read the clues, then write the words.
Start at the bottom and climb to the top.

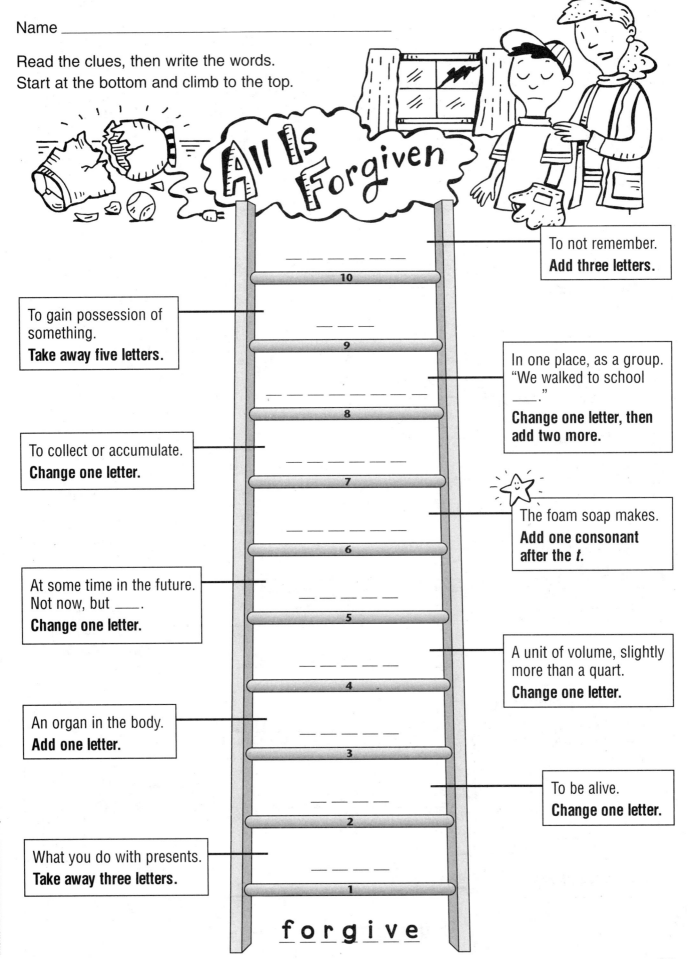

All Is Forgiven

To not remember.
Add three letters.

_ _ _ _ _ _ _   10

To gain possession of
something.
Take away five letters.

_ _ _   9

In one place, as a group.
"We walked to school
____."
**Change one letter, then
add two more.**

_ _ _ _ _ _ _   8

To collect or accumulate.
Change one letter.

_ _ _ _ _ _   7

The foam soap makes.
**Add one consonant
after the _t_.**

_ _ _ _ _   6

At some time in the future.
Not now, but ____.
Change one letter.

_ _ _ _ _   5

A unit of volume, slightly
more than a quart.
Change one letter.

_ _ _ _ _   4

An organ in the body.
Add one letter.

_ _ _ _   3

To be alive.
Change one letter.

_ _ _ _   2

What you do with presents.
Take away three letters.

_ _ _ _   1

f o r g i v e

Name _____

Read the clues, then write the words.
Start at the bottom and climb to the top.

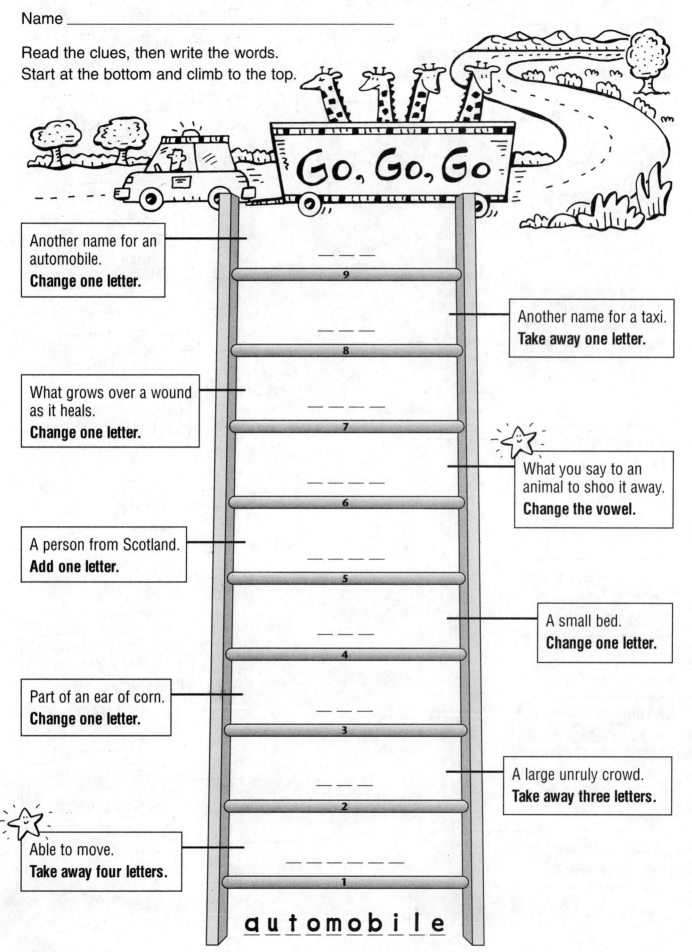

Go, Go, Go

Another name for an automobile.
Change one letter.

___ ___ ___ ___
9

Another name for a taxi.
Take away one letter.

___ ___ ___
8

What grows over a wound as it heals.
Change one letter.

___ ___ ___ ___
7

What you say to an animal to shoo it away.
Change the vowel.

___ ___ ___ ___
6

A person from Scotland.
Add one letter.

___ ___ ___ ___ ___
5

A small bed.
Change one letter.

___ ___ ___
4

Part of an ear of corn.
Change one letter.

___ ___ ___
3

A large unruly crowd.
Take away three letters.

___ ___ ___
2

Able to move.
Take away four letters.

___ ___ ___ ___ ___ ___
1

a u t o m o b i l e

Interactive Whiteboard Activities: Daily Word Ladders Grades 4–6 © 2012 Timothy V. Rasinski, Scholastic Teaching Resources

Name _____

Read the clues, then write the words.
Start at the bottom and climb to the top.

All in the Family

Your uncle is married to your ___.
Add one letter.

An insect that lives in a colony.
Change one letter.

Music, sculpture, painting, dance, etc.
Change one letter.

"We ___ going to school today."
Rearrange the letters.

A part of the head used for hearing.
Take away four letters.

Serious and eager.
Add three letters to the end.

To make money through work.
Take away one letter.

To gain knowledge.
Take away one letter, then add one.

Transparent.
Take away two letters.

Relating to atomic energy.
Rearrange the first two letters.

Not clear.
Add two letters.

11

10

9

8

7

6

5

4

3

2

1

u n c l e

Interactive Whiteboard Activities: Daily Word Ladders Grades 4–6 © 2012 Timothy V. Rasinski, Scholastic Teaching Resources

Name _____

Read the clues, then write the words.
Start at the bottom and climb to the top.

Give a Dog a Bone

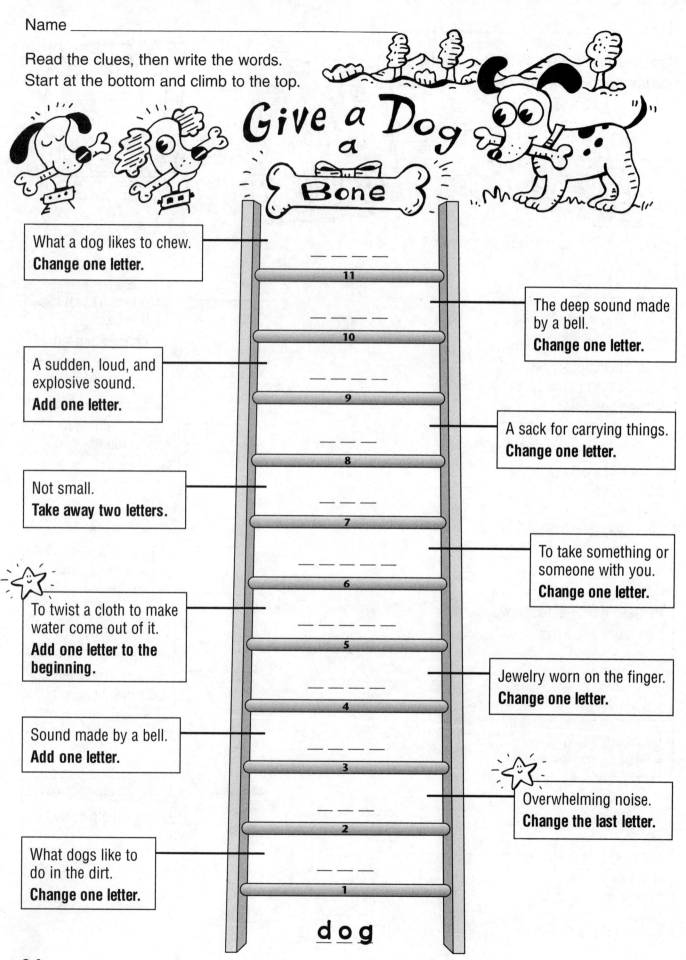

What a dog likes to chew.
Change one letter.

The deep sound made by a bell.
Change one letter.

A sudden, loud, and explosive sound.
Add one letter.

A sack for carrying things.
Change one letter.

Not small.
Take away two letters.

To take something or someone with you.
Change one letter.

To twist a cloth to make water come out of it.
Add one letter to the beginning.

Jewelry worn on the finger.
Change one letter.

Sound made by a bell.
Add one letter.

Overwhelming noise.
Change the last letter.

What dogs like to do in the dirt.
Change one letter.

11
10
9
8
7
6
5
4
3
2
1

d o g

Interactive Whiteboard Activities: Daily Word Ladders Grades 4–6 © 2012 Timothy V. Rasinski, Scholastic Teaching Resources

Name _____

Read the clues, then write the words.
Start at the bottom and climb to the top.

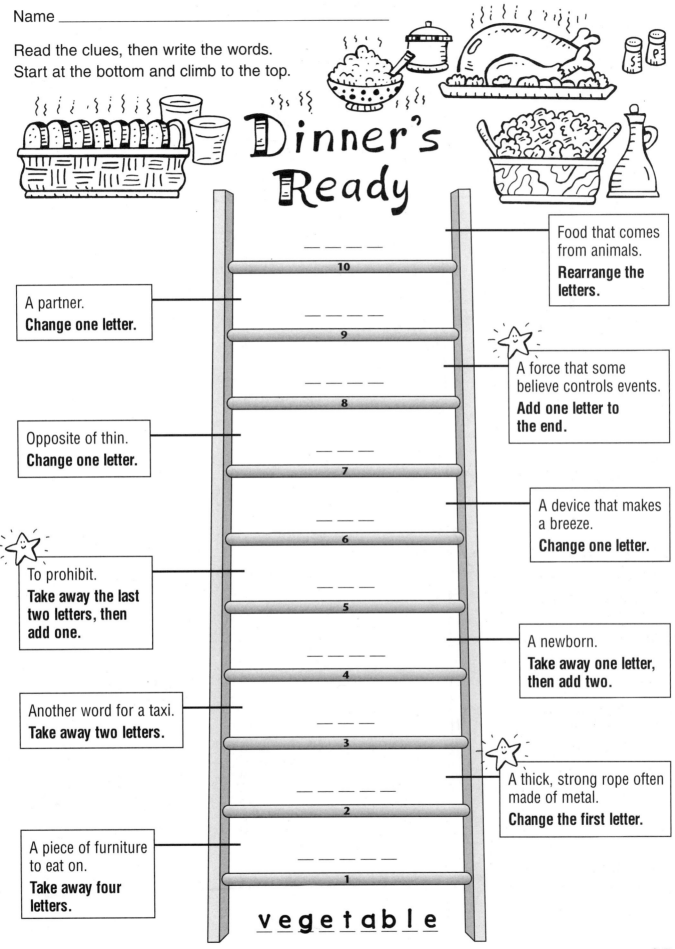

Dinner's Ready

Food that comes from animals.
Rearrange the letters.

A partner.
Change one letter.

A force that some believe controls events.
Add one letter to the end.

Opposite of thin.
Change one letter.

A device that makes a breeze.
Change one letter.

To prohibit.
Take away the last two letters, then add one.

A newborn.
Take away one letter, then add two.

Another word for a taxi.
Take away two letters.

A thick, strong rope often made of metal.
Change the first letter.

A piece of furniture to eat on.
Take away four letters.

v e g e t a b l e

Name _____

Read the clues, then write the words.
Start at the bottom and climb to the top.

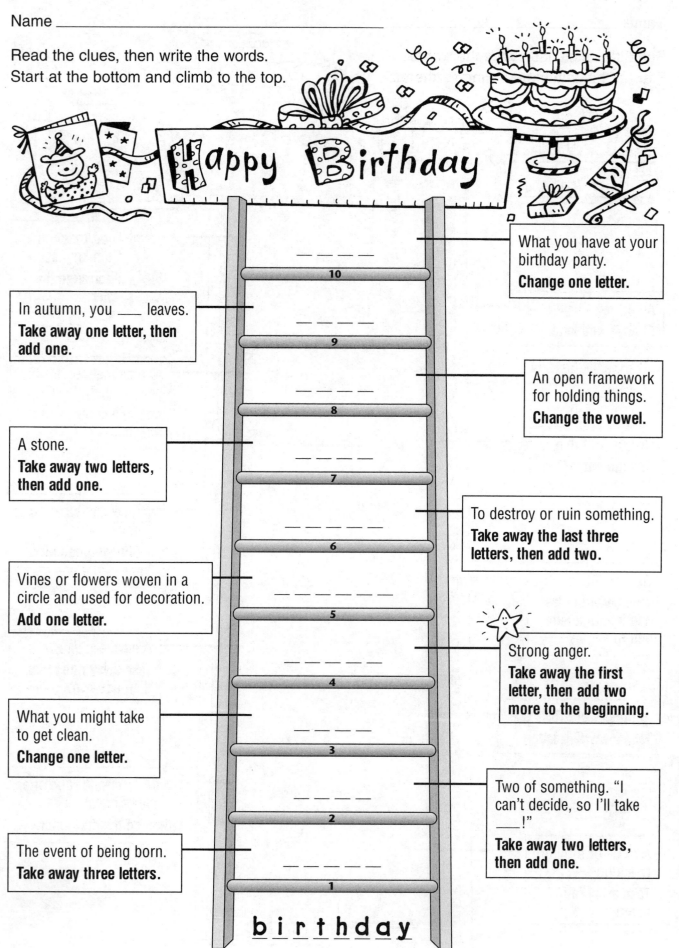

Happy Birthday

What you have at your birthday party.
Change one letter.

10 _ _ _ _ _

In autumn, you ___ leaves.
Take away one letter, then add one.

9 _ _ _ _ _

An open framework for holding things.
Change the vowel.

8 _ _ _ _ _

A stone.
Take away two letters, then add one.

7 _ _ _ _ _

To destroy or ruin something.
Take away the last three letters, then add two.

6 _ _ _ _ _ _

Vines or flowers woven in a circle and used for decoration.
Add one letter.

5 _ _ _ _ _ _ _

Strong anger.
Take away the first letter, then add two more to the beginning.

4 _ _ _ _ _ _

What you might take to get clean.
Change one letter.

3 _ _ _ _

Two of something. "I can't decide, so I'll take ___!"
Take away two letters, then add one.

2 _ _ _ _ _

The event of being born.
Take away three letters.

1 _ _ _ _ _ _

b i r t h d a y

Interactive Whiteboard Activities: Daily Word Ladders Grades 4–6 © 2012 Timothy V. Rasinski, Scholastic Teaching Resources

Name _____

Read the clues, then write the words.
Start at the bottom and climb to the top.

Chew on This

10. _ _ _ _ _ — What you do after you take a bite. **Change one letter.**

9. _ _ _ _ — A ___ is a kind of dog with a blue tongue. Also, another word for food. **Change the last letter.**

8. _ _ _ _ _ — To cut with a quick blow. **Add one letter.**

7. _ _ _ — To move by taking small jumps. **Take away one letter.**

6. _ _ _ _ — To go to stores and buy things. **Change one letter.**

5. _ _ _ _ — "Ouch! The doctor gave me a ___." **Change one letter.**

4. _ _ _ _ — To close. **Add one letter.**

3. _ _ _ — A small house or dwelling. **Change one letter.**

2. _ _ _ _ — "I got a sled for my birthday, ___ I wanted a bike." **Change one letter.**

1. _ _ _ _ — Gripped with your teeth. **Take away one letter.**

b i t e

Name _____

Read the clues, then write the words.
Start at the bottom and climb to the top.

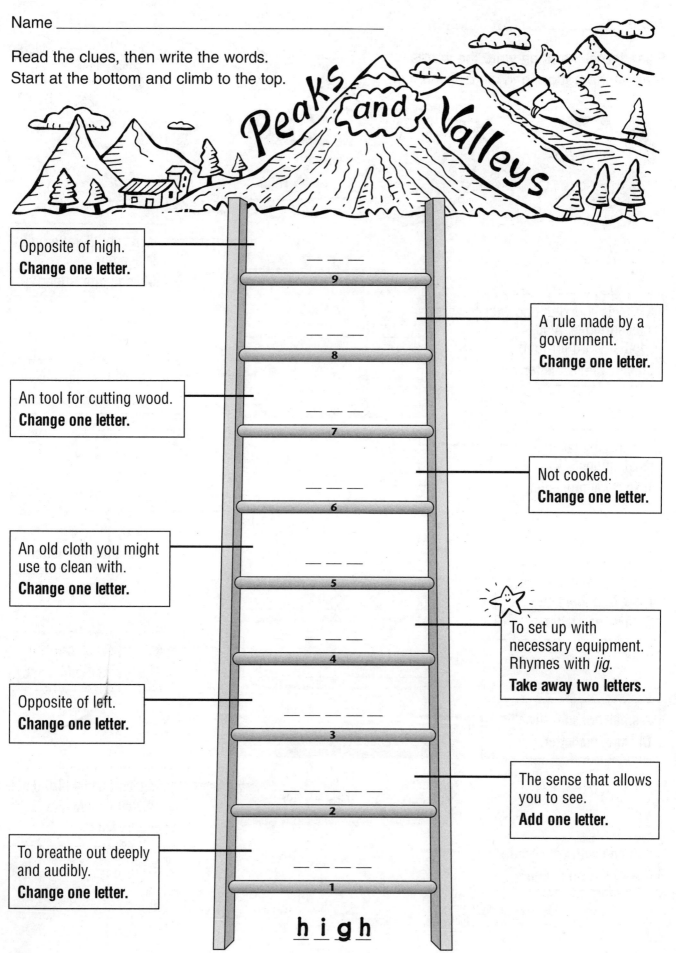

Peaks and Valleys

Opposite of high.
Change one letter.
— — — — 9

A rule made by a government.
Change one letter.
— — — — 8

An tool for cutting wood.
Change one letter.
— — — — 7

Not cooked.
Change one letter.
— — — — 6

An old cloth you might use to clean with.
Change one letter.
— — — — 5

To set up with necessary equipment. Rhymes with *jig*.
Take away two letters.
— — — 4

Opposite of left.
Change one letter.
— — — — — 3

The sense that allows you to see.
Add one letter.
— — — — — 2

To breathe out deeply and audibly.
Change one letter.
— — — — — 1

h i g h

38

Interactive Whiteboard Activities: Daily Word Ladders Grades 4–6 © 2012 Timothy V. Rasinski, Scholastic Teaching Resources

Name _____

Read the clues, then write the words.
Start at the bottom and climb to the top.

A Rose Is a Rose

A type of flower.
Change one letter.

What you use for smelling and breathing.
Change one letter.

A short letter or message.
Take away one letter, then add one.

A fastening you make in string or rope.
Add one letter.

This word makes a statement negative.
Change one letter.

Plenty of something.
Take away one letter.

A small, narrow opening.
"Put the coin in the ___."
Change the last letter.

Opposite of fast.
Add one letter.

Opposite of high.
Take away two letters.

Bring down. "The elevator ___ed us to the first floor."
Take away one letter.

10 _ _ _ _ _
9 _ _ _ _
8 _ _ _ _
7 _ _ _ _ _
6 _ _ _
5 _ _ _
4 _ _ _ _
3 _ _ _ _
2 _ _ _
1 _ _ _ _ _

f l o w e r

Name _____

Read the clues, then write the words.
Start at the bottom and climb to the top.

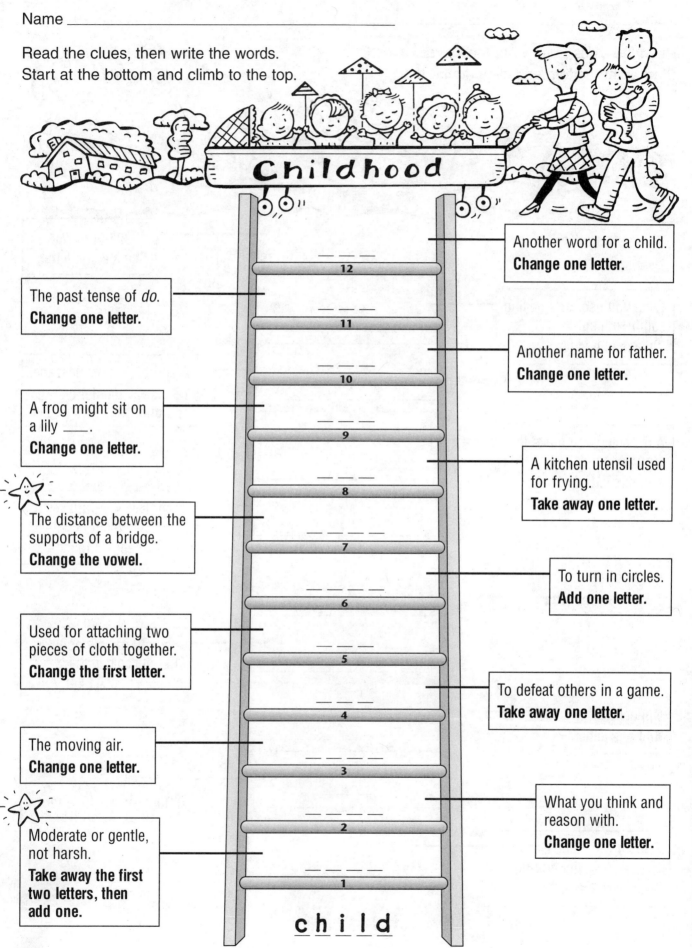

Childhood

Another word for a child.
Change one letter.

The past tense of *do*.
Change one letter.

Another name for father.
Change one letter.

A frog might sit on
a lily ___.
Change one letter.

A kitchen utensil used
for frying.
Take away one letter.

The distance between the
supports of a bridge.
Change the vowel.

To turn in circles.
Add one letter.

Used for attaching two
pieces of cloth together.
Change the first letter.

To defeat others in a game.
Take away one letter.

The moving air.
Change one letter.

What you think and
reason with.
Change one letter.

Moderate or gentle,
not harsh.
**Take away the first
two letters, then
add one.**

12
11
10
9
8
7
6
5
4
3
2
1

c h i l d

Interactive Whiteboard Activities: Daily Word Ladders Grades 4–6 © 2012 Timothy V. Rasinski, Scholastic Teaching Resources

Name _____

Read the clues, then write the words.
Start at the bottom and climb to the top.

Cheese Eaters

A large rodent.
Change one letter.

_ _ _

9

A nocturnal flying mammal.
Take away one letter.

8

What you might take
to get clean.
Change one letter.

_ _ _ _

7

To hit with crushing force.
Rhymes with *lash*.
Change one letter.

_ _ _ _

6

The foundation of something.
**Take away the first two
letters, then add one.**

_ _ _ _

5

To pursue or hunt.
Change one letter.

_ _ _ _

4

Picked something.
**Add one letter to the
beginning.**

_ _ _ _

3

A long hollow tube for
carrying water.
Take away one letter.

_ _ _ _ _

2

A place to live.
Change one letter.

_ _ _ _ _

1

m o u s e

Name _____

Read the clues, then write the words.
Start at the bottom and climb to the top.

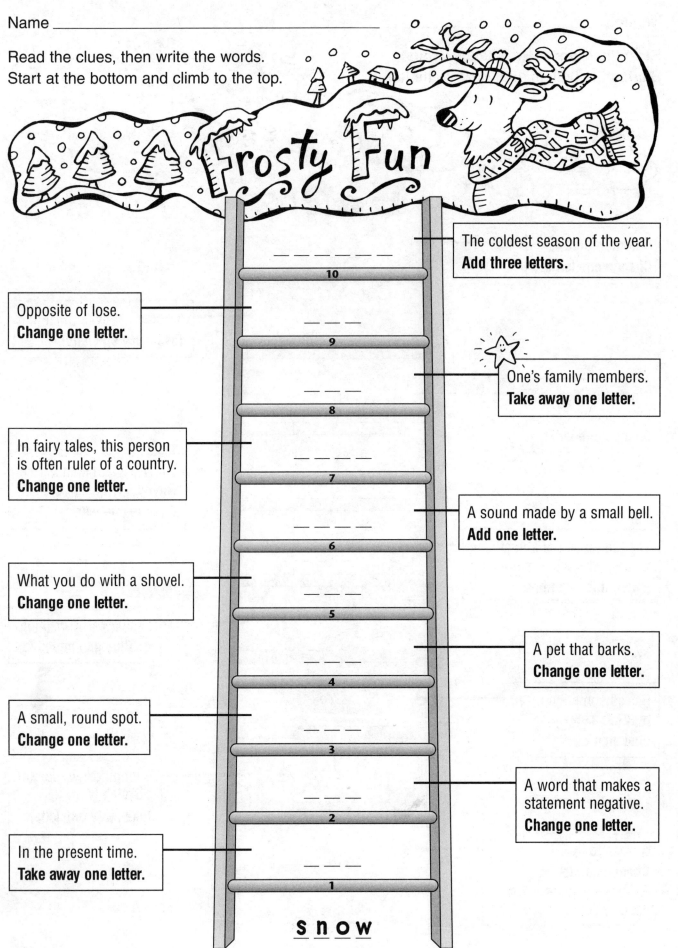

Frosty Fun

The coldest season of the year.
Add three letters.

_ _ _ _ _ _

10

Opposite of lose.
Change one letter.

_ _ _

9

One's family members.
Take away one letter.

_ _ _

8

In fairy tales, this person
is often ruler of a country.
Change one letter.

_ _ _ _

7

A sound made by a small bell.
Add one letter.

_ _ _ _

6

What you do with a shovel.
Change one letter.

_ _ _

5

A pet that barks.
Change one letter.

_ _ _

4

A small, round spot.
Change one letter.

_ _ _

3

A word that makes a
statement negative.
Change one letter.

_ _ _

2

In the present time.
Take away one letter.

_ _ _

1

s n o w

Interactive Whiteboard Activities: Daily Word Ladders Grades 4–6 © 2012 Timothy V. Rasinski, Scholastic Teaching Resources

Name _____

Read the clues, then write the words.
Start at the bottom and climb to the top.

Seaworthy

Another word for ocean.
Take away one letter.

_ _ _ _
9

An ocean mammal
with flippers.
Change one letter.

_ _ _ _ _
8

You sit on this.
Change one letter.

_ _ _ _ _
7

This makes something hot.
Take away one letter.

_ _ _ _ _
6

Body organ that
pumps blood.
Change one letter.

_ _ _ _ _
5

Listened to something.
Change one letter.

_ _ _ _ _
4

Hair that grows on
a man's face.
Add one letter.

_ _ _ _
3

A small ball that can
go on a necklace.
Change one letter.

_ _ _ _
2

The edible seed of certain
plants.
**Take away the first two
letters, then add one.**

_ _ _ _ _
1

o c e a n

Interactive Whiteboard Activities: Daily Word Ladders Grades 4–6 © 2012 Timothy V. Rasinski, Scholastic Teaching Resources

Name _____

Read the clues, then write the words.
Start at the bottom and climb to the top.

What you do with a needle while sewing.
Add two letters at the beginning.

This makes you want to scratch.
Take away one letter.

A costume you might see on Halloween.
Add two letters.

Cleverness or intelligence.
Take away one letter.

What plants do without water.
Change one letter.

A short plaid skirt sometimes worn by Scotsmen.
Change one letter.

To end or destroy.
Take away one letter.

Expert ability at doing something.
Change one letter.

Quiet and unmoving.
Add one letter.

Wood or stone that runs along the bottom of a door or window.
Change the vowel.

What stores do with the things in them.
Take away the last letter, then add two.

11 _ _ _ _ _ _ _

10 _ _ _ _ _

9 _ _ _ _ _

8 _ _ _ _

7 _ _ _ _ _

6 _ _ _ _ _

5 _ _ _ _ _

4 _ _ _ _ _

3 _ _ _ _ _

2 _ _ _ _

1 _ _ _ _

s e w

44

Interactive Whiteboard Activities: Daily Word Ladders Grades 4–6 © 2012 Timothy V. Rasinski, Scholastic Teaching Resources

Name _____

Read the clues, then write the words.
Start at the bottom and climb to the top.

Save Your Pennies

A homophone of the previous word. A penny is worth one ___.
Change one letter.

Caused something to go.
Change the last letter.

To cause something to go somewhere.
Change one letter.

You plant this in the ground.
Take away one letter.

The rate at which something moves.
Change one letter.

"I hope to ___ no more than ten dollars at the movie."
Take away the first letter, then add two.

Opposite of closed.
Rearrange the letters.

A slang word for *no.*
Add an *o*, then rearrange.

An instrument for writing.
Take away two letters.

9 _ _ _ _ _

8 _ _ _ _

7 _ _ _ _

6 _ _ _ _

5 _ _ _ _ _

4 _ _ _ _ _

3 _ _ _ _

2 _ _ _ _

1 _ _ _

p e n n y

Interactive Whiteboard Activities: Daily Word Ladders Grades 4–6 © 2012 Timothy V. Rasinski, Scholastic Teaching Resources

Name _____

Read the clues, then write the words.
Start at the bottom and climb to the top.

Right   or   Wrong

Not true.
Take away the last letter, then add two.

_ _ _ _ _   10

The season before winter.
Change one letter.

_ _ _ _   9

A corridor or passageway in a building.
Take away the last letter, then add two.

_ _ _ _   8

A meat that comes from pigs.
Change one letter.

_ _ _   7

To sing a melody with your mouth closed
Change one letter.

_ _ _ _   6

The center part of a wheel or circle.
Change the first letter.

_ _ _ _   5

A young bear.
Take away one letter.

_ _ _ _   4

An association of people who have something in common.
Change one letter.

_ _ _ _ _   3

A piece of evidence used to solve a mystery or problem.
Change one letter.

_ _ _ _   2

A color.
Change the first two letters.

_ _ _ _   1

t r u e

Interactive Whiteboard Activities: Daily Word Ladders Grades 4–6 © 2012 Timothy V. Rasinski, Scholastic Teaching Resources

Name _____

Read the clues, then write the words.
Start at the bottom and climb to the top.

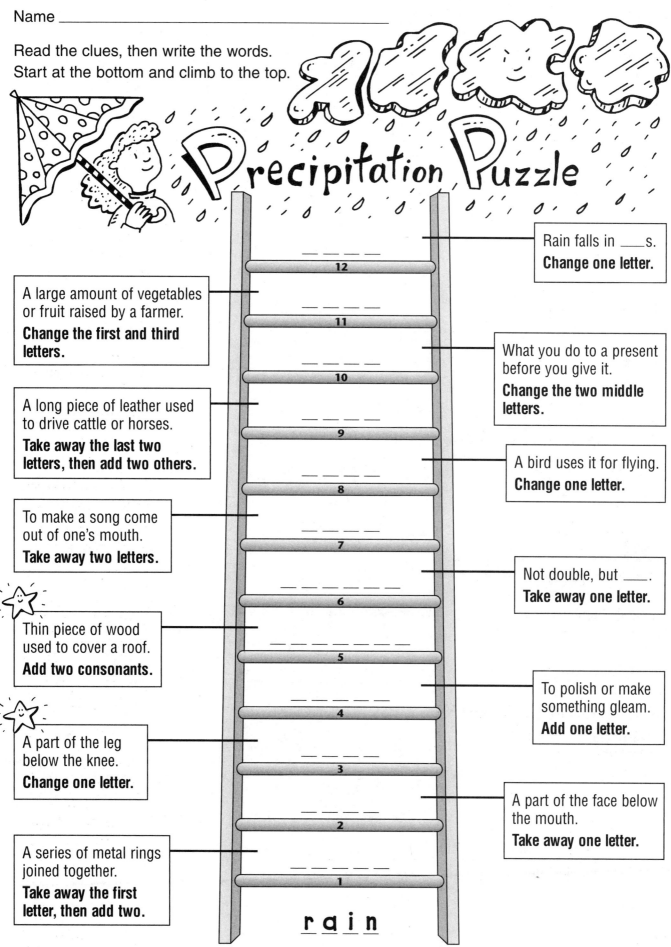

Precipitation Puzzle

Rain falls in ___s.
Change one letter.

A large amount of vegetables or fruit raised by a farmer.
Change the first and third letters.

What you do to a present before you give it.
Change the two middle letters.

A long piece of leather used to drive cattle or horses.
Take away the last two letters, then add two others.

A bird uses it for flying.
Change one letter.

To make a song come out of one's mouth.
Take away two letters.

Not double, but ___.
Take away one letter.

Thin piece of wood used to cover a roof.
Add two consonants.

To polish or make something gleam.
Add one letter.

A part of the leg below the knee.
Change one letter.

A part of the face below the mouth.
Take away one letter.

A series of metal rings joined together.
Take away the first letter, then add two.

12
11
10
9
8
7
6
5
4
3
2
1

r a i n

Interactive Whiteboard Activities: Daily Word Ladders Grades 4–6 © 2012 Timothy V. Rasinski, Scholastic Teaching Resources

Name _____

Read the clues, then write the words.
Start at the bottom and climb to the top.

Snow Day

What can fall from the sky in winter.
Add one letter.

10 _ _ _ _ _

In the present time.
Change one letter.

9 _ _ _

A series of things in a straight line.
Take away one letter.

8 _ _ _

To get larger.
Change the last two letters.

7 _ _ _ _ _

A kind of smile.
Take away one letter.

6 _ _ _ _ _

A tiny hard particle, as in "a ___ of sand or wheat."
Add one letter.

5 _ _ _ _ _

Precipitation.
Change one letter.

4 _ _ _ _

What a train rides on.
Rearrange the letters.

3 _ _ _ _

Someone who doesn't tell the truth.
Take away two letters.

2 _ _ _ _ _

A small four-legged reptile.
Take away two letters.

1 b l i z z a r d

Interactive Whiteboard Activities: Daily Word Ladders Grades 4–6 © 2012 Timothy V. Rasinski, Scholastic Teaching Resources

Name _____

Read the clues, then write the words.
Start at the bottom and climb to the top.

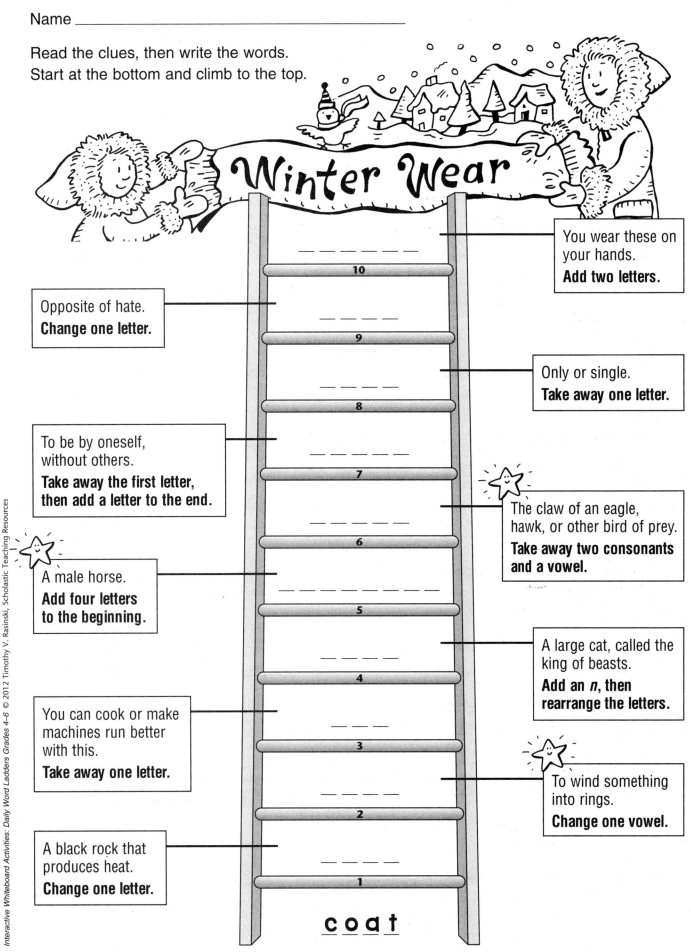

Winter Wear

You wear these on your hands.
Add two letters.

Opposite of hate.
Change one letter.

Only or single.
Take away one letter.

To be by oneself, without others.
Take away the first letter, then add a letter to the end.

The claw of an eagle, hawk, or other bird of prey.
Take away two consonants and a vowel.

A male horse.
Add four letters to the beginning.

A large cat, called the king of beasts.
Add an *n*, then rearrange the letters.

You can cook or make machines run better with this.
Take away one letter.

To wind something into rings.
Change one vowel.

A black rock that produces heat.
Change one letter.

10

9

8

7

6

5

4

3

2

1

c o a t

Interactive Whiteboard Activities: Daily Word Ladders Grades 4–6 © 2012 Timothy V. Rasinski, Scholastic Teaching Resources

Name _____

Read the clues, then write the words.
Start at the bottom and climb to the top.

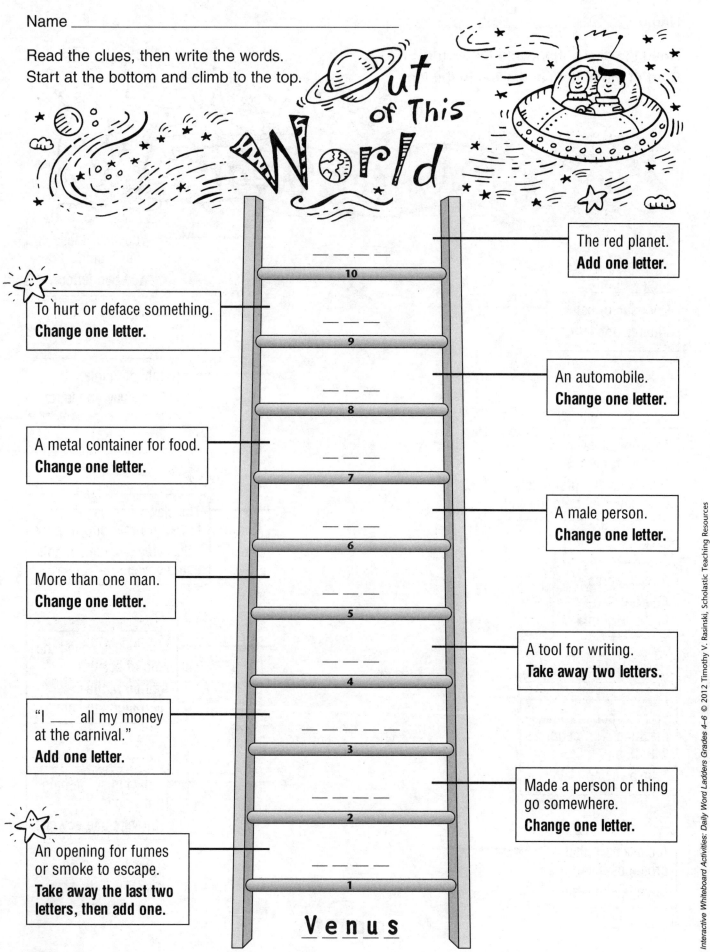

Out of This World

The red planet.
Add one letter.

_ _ _ _ _
10

To hurt or deface something.
Change one letter.

_ _ _ _
9

An automobile.
Change one letter.

_ _ _ _
8

A metal container for food.
Change one letter.

_ _ _ _
7

A male person.
Change one letter.

_ _ _ _
6

More than one man.
Change one letter.

_ _ _ _
5

A tool for writing.
Take away two letters.

_ _ _
4

"I ___ all my money at the carnival."
Add one letter.

_ _ _ _ _
3

Made a person or thing go somewhere.
Change one letter.

_ _ _ _
2

An opening for fumes or smoke to escape.
Take away the last two letters, then add one.

_ _ _ _
1

V e n u s

50

Interactive Whiteboard Activities: Daily Word Ladders Grades 4–6 © 2012 Timothy V. Rasinski, Scholastic Teaching Resources

Name _____

Read the clues, then write the words.
Start at the bottom and climb to the top.

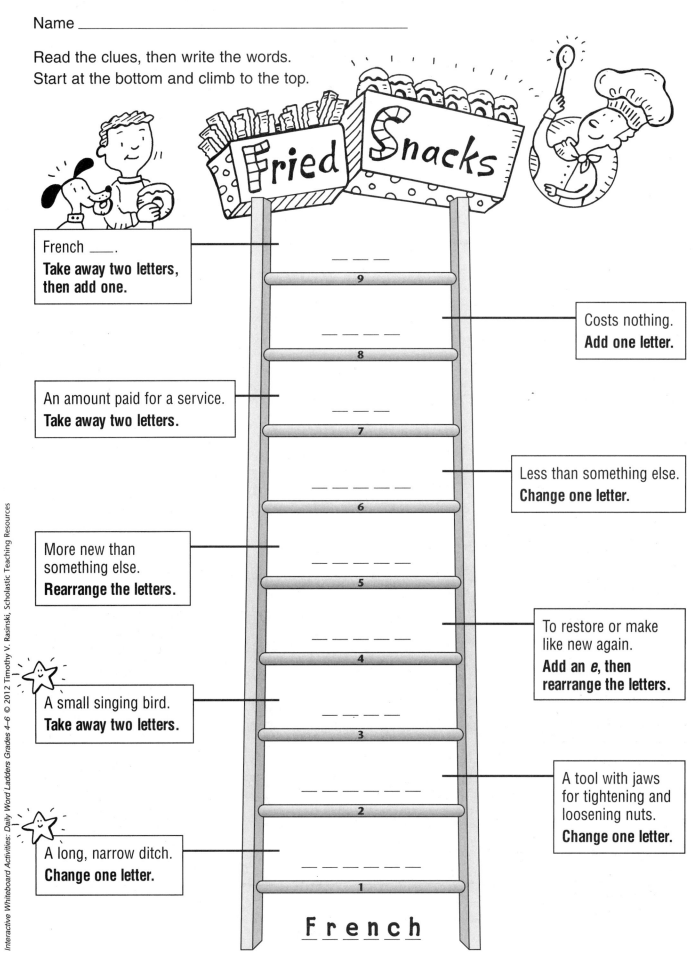

French ___.
Take away two letters, then add one.

9 _ _ _ _

Costs nothing.
Add one letter.

8 _ _ _ _

An amount paid for a service.
Take away two letters.

7 _ _ _

Less than something else.
Change one letter.

6 _ _ _ _ _

More new than something else.
Rearrange the letters.

5 _ _ _ _ _

To restore or make like new again.
Add an *e*, then rearrange the letters.

4 _ _ _ _ _

A small singing bird.
Take away two letters.

3 _ _ _ _

A tool with jaws for tightening and loosening nuts.
Change one letter.

2 _ _ _ _ _ _

A long, narrow ditch.
Change one letter.

1 _ _ _ _ _ _

F r e n c h

Name _____

Read the clues, then write the words.
Start at the bottom and climb to the top.

Candlelight

Clue	Rung
What is made by a lit candle. **Change one letter.**	9
To shine with a sudden light. **Add one letter after the _f_.**	8
The cost of traveling on a bus, plane, or subway. **Change one letter.**	7
Another name for a rabbit. **Take away one letter.**	6
To give to others some of what you have. **Change one letter.**	5
A small piece or part of something, like a piece of glass. **Add one letter to the beginning.**	4
Not soft. **Change one letter.**	3
What's attached to the end of your arm. **Take away two letters.**	2
The part of an object that you hold. **Change one letter.**	1

c a n d l e

Name _____

Read the clues, then write the words.
Start at the bottom and climb to the top.

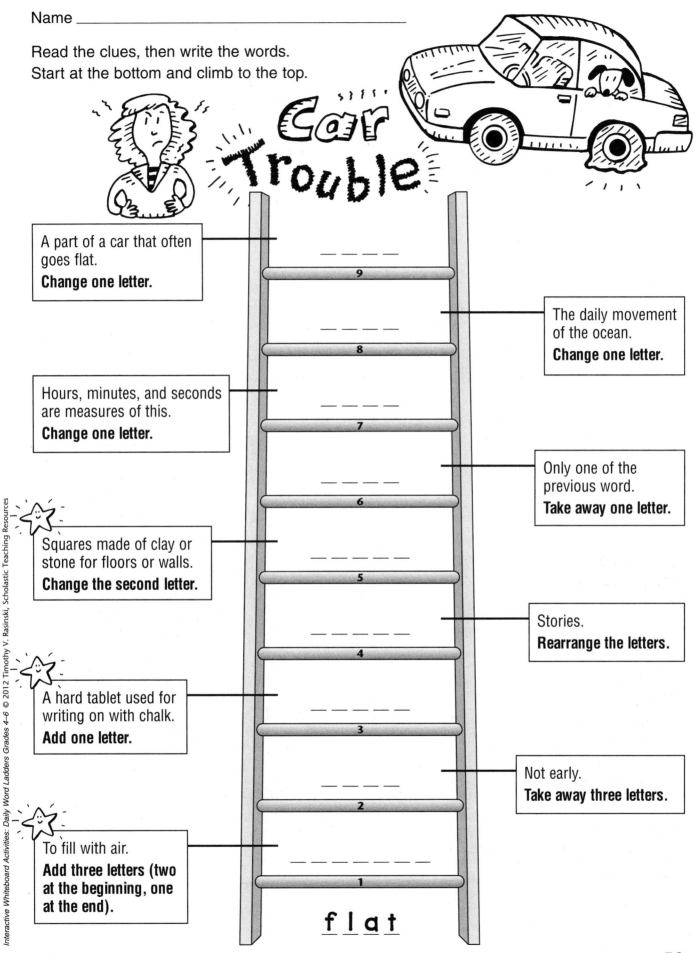

A part of a car that often goes flat.
Change one letter.

The daily movement of the ocean.
Change one letter.

Hours, minutes, and seconds are measures of this.
Change one letter.

Only one of the previous word.
Take away one letter.

Squares made of clay or stone for floors or walls.
Change the second letter.

Stories.
Rearrange the letters.

A hard tablet used for writing on with chalk.
Add one letter.

Not early.
Take away three letters.

To fill with air.
Add three letters (two at the beginning, one at the end).

9
8
7
6
5
4
3
2
1

f l a t

Interactive Whiteboard Activities: Daily Word Ladders Grades 4–6 © 2012 Timothy V. Rasinski, Scholastic Teaching Resources

Name _____

Read the clues, then write the words.
Start at the bottom and climb to the top.

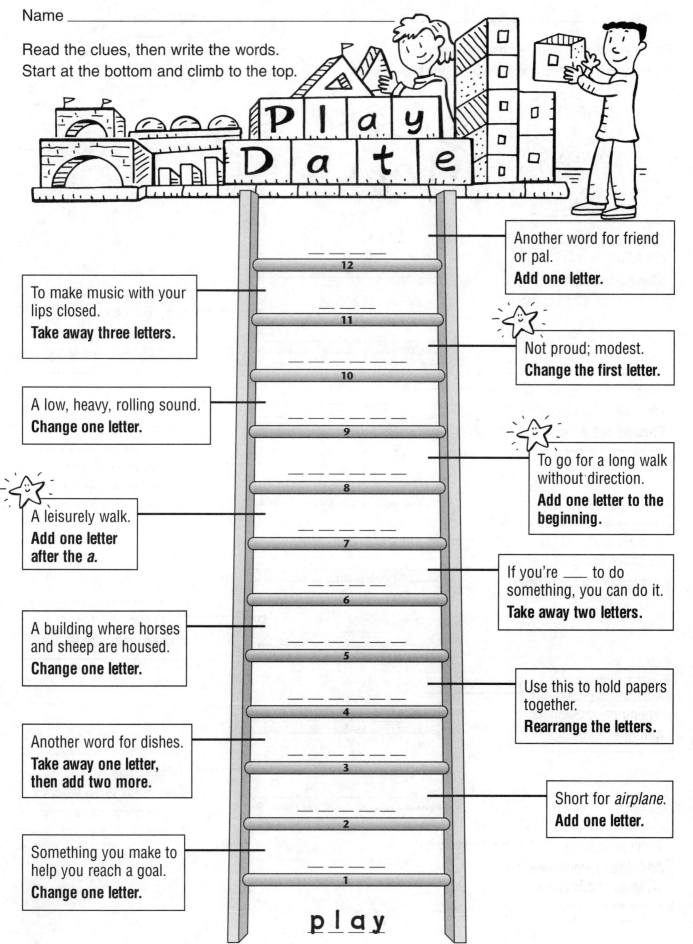

Another word for friend or pal.
Add one letter.

To make music with your lips closed.
Take away three letters.

Not proud; modest.
Change the first letter.

A low, heavy, rolling sound.
Change one letter.

To go for a long walk without direction.
Add one letter to the beginning.

A leisurely walk.
Add one letter after the _a_.

If you're ___ to do something, you can do it.
Take away two letters.

A building where horses and sheep are housed.
Change one letter.

Use this to hold papers together.
Rearrange the letters.

Another word for dishes.
Take away one letter, then add two more.

Short for _airplane_.
Add one letter.

Something you make to help you reach a goal.
Change one letter.

12
11
10
9
8
7
6
5
4
3
2
1

p l a y

54

Interactive Whiteboard Activities: Daily Word Ladders Grades 4–6 © 2012 Timothy V. Rasinski, Scholastic Teaching Resources

Name _____

Read the clues, then write the words.
Start at the bottom and climb to the top.

Beautiful Day

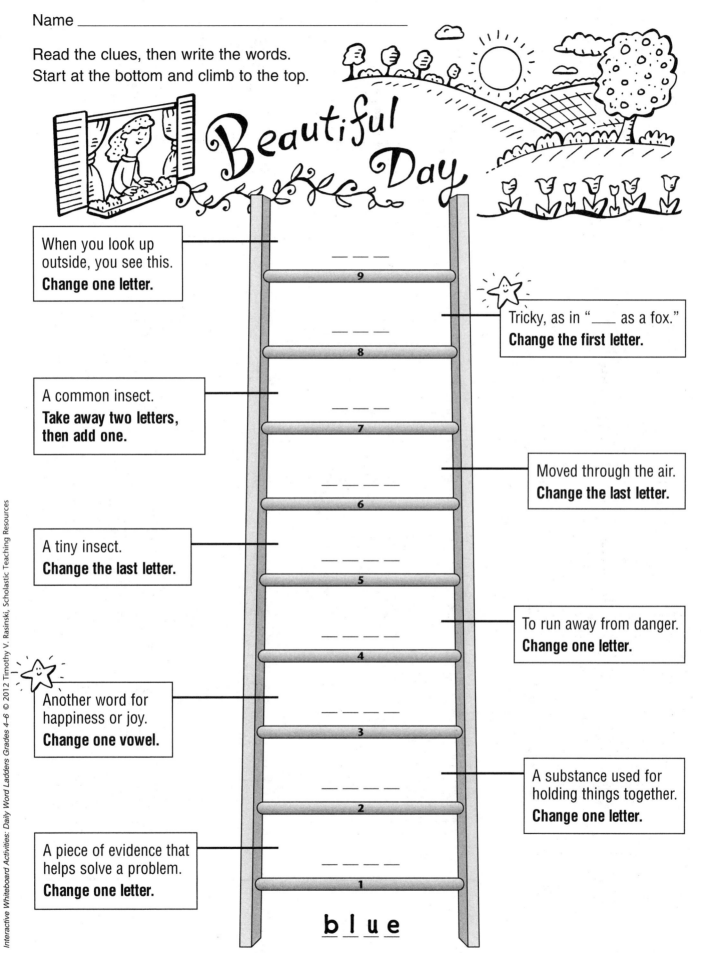

When you look up outside, you see this.
Change one letter.
9. _ _ _

Tricky, as in "___ as a fox."
Change the first letter.
8. _ _ _

A common insect.
Take away two letters, then add one.
7. _ _ _

Moved through the air.
Change the last letter.
6. _ _ _ _

A tiny insect.
Change the last letter.
5. _ _ _ _

To run away from danger.
Change one letter.
4. _ _ _ _

Another word for happiness or joy.
Change one vowel.
3. _ _ _ _

A substance used for holding things together.
Change one letter.
2. _ _ _ _

A piece of evidence that helps solve a problem.
Change one letter.
1. _ _ _ _

b l u e

Name _____

Read the clues, then write the words.
Start at the bottom and climb to the top.

Ruling the Roost

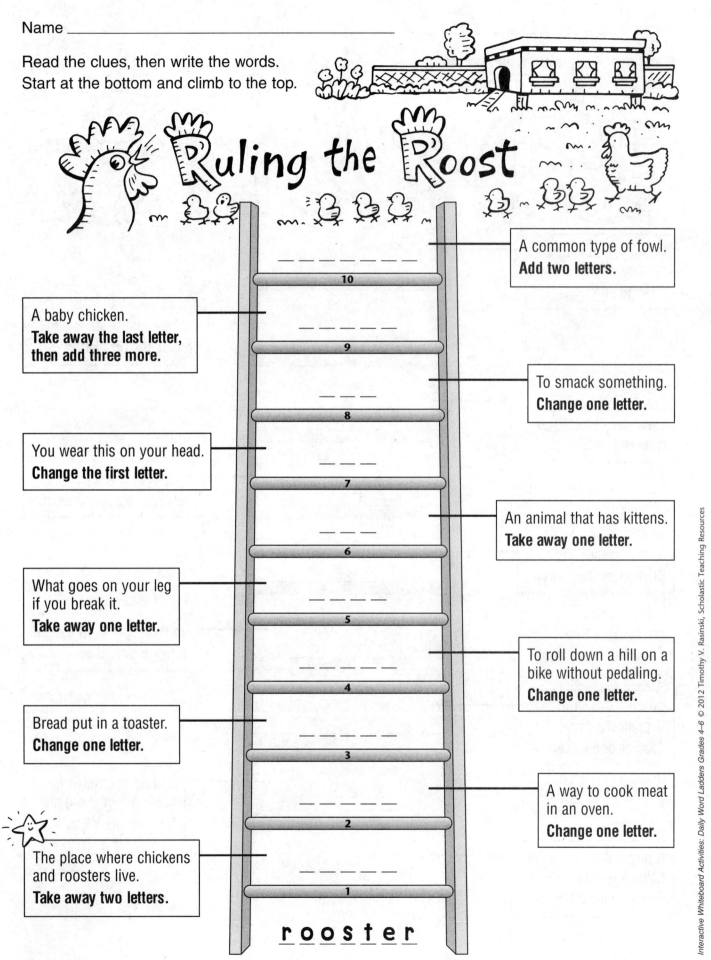

A common type of fowl.
Add two letters.

_ _ _ _ _ _ _
10

A baby chicken.
**Take away the last letter,
then add three more.**

_ _ _ _ _ _
9

To smack something.
Change one letter.

_ _ _ _
8

You wear this on your head.
Change the first letter.

_ _ _ _
7

An animal that has kittens.
Take away one letter.

_ _ _ _
6

What goes on your leg
if you break it.
Take away one letter.

_ _ _ _ _
5

To roll down a hill on a
bike without pedaling.
Change one letter.

_ _ _ _ _ _
4

Bread put in a toaster.
Change one letter.

_ _ _ _ _ _
3

A way to cook meat
in an oven.
Change one letter.

_ _ _ _ _ _
2

The place where chickens
and roosters live.
Take away two letters.

_ _ _ _ _ _
1

r o o s t e r

Interactive Whiteboard Activities: Daily Word Ladders Grades 4–6 © 2012 Timothy V. Rasinski, Scholastic Teaching Resources

Name _____

Read the clues, then write the words.
Start at the bottom and climb to the top.

New and Not-So-New

Opposite of new.
Take away one letter, then add one.

— — —   11

A bird of prey active at night.
Change one letter.

— — —   10

To possess or have something.
Take away two letters.

— — —   9

To have exhibited something to others in the past.
Add one letter.

— — — — —   8

To exhibit something to others.
Add one letter.

— — — —   7

"___ are you?"
Change the first letter.

— — —   6

In the present.
Change one letter.

— — —   5

An adult female pig.
Change the middle letter.

— — —   4

To fasten material with needle and thread.
Change one letter.

— — —   3

Moisture on grass early in the morning.
Change one letter.

— — —   2

Not many.
Change one letter.

— — —   1

n e w

Name _____

Read the clues, then write the words.
Start at the bottom and climb to the top.

Midday Meal

Another word for dinner.
Change one letter.

_ _ _ _ _ _
9

Someone who sips.
Add three letters.

_ _ _ _ _ _
8

To drink in small amounts.
Change one letter.

_ _ _ _
7

A liquid that comes from a tree.
Change one letter.

_ _ _
6

To speak.
Change one letter.

_ _ _ _
5

Opposite of night.
Change one letter.

_ _ _
4

Not wet.
Take away four letters.

_ _ _
3

Where you put dirty clothes.
Take away the last two letters, then add three.

_ _ _ _ _ _ _
2

What you do to send a rocket into space.
Add one vowel.

_ _ _ _ _ _
1

l u n c h

Interactive Whiteboard Activities: Daily Word Ladders Grades 4–6 © 2012 Timothy V. Rasinski, Scholastic Teaching Resources

Name _____

Read the clues, then write the words.
Start at the bottom and climb to the top.

Growing Up

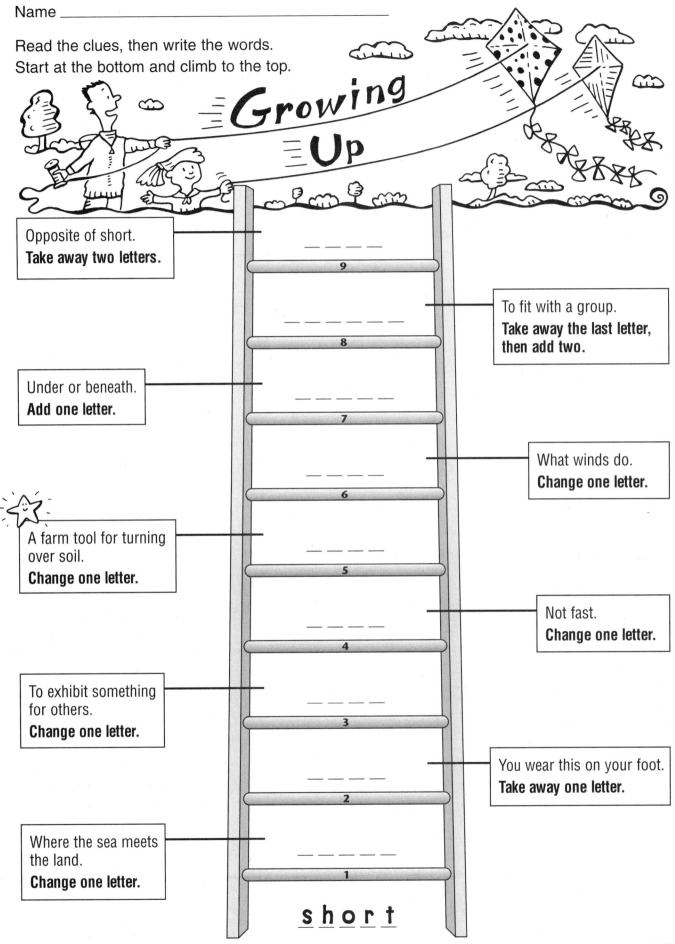

Opposite of short.
Take away two letters.

To fit with a group.
Take away the last letter, then add two.

Under or beneath.
Add one letter.

What winds do.
Change one letter.

A farm tool for turning over soil.
Change one letter.

Not fast.
Change one letter.

To exhibit something for others.
Change one letter.

You wear this on your foot.
Take away one letter.

Where the sea meets the land.
Change one letter.

9
8
7
6
5
4
3
2
1

s h o r t

Interactive Whiteboard Activities: Daily Word Ladders Grades 4–6 © 2012 Timothy V. Rasinski, Scholastic Teaching Resources

Name _____

Read the clues, then write the words.
Start at the bottom and climb to the top.

Wedding Words

The partner of a bride.
Add one letter.

9 _ _ _ _ _ _

A section of a house
or building.
Change one letter.

8 _ _ _ _ _

To go from place to place;
to wander.
Change one letter.

7 _ _ _ _ _

Another word for
street or path.
**Take away one letter,
then add one.**

6 _ _ _ _ _

To have ridden on something.
Add one letter.

5 _ _ _ _ _

A long, thin stick.
Change the vowel.

4 _ _ _ _

To remove something, as
in "Get ___ of that junk."
Take away one letter.

3 _ _ _

To travel on an animal
or in a vehicle.
Take away two letters.

2 _ _ _ _ _

To walk, taking large steps.
**Take away the first letter,
then add two.**

1 _ _ _ _ _ _

b r i d e

Interactive Whiteboard Activities: Daily Word Ladders Grades 4–6 © 2012 Timothy V. Rasinski, Scholastic Teaching Resources

Name _____

Read the clues, then write the words.
Start at the bottom and climb to the top.

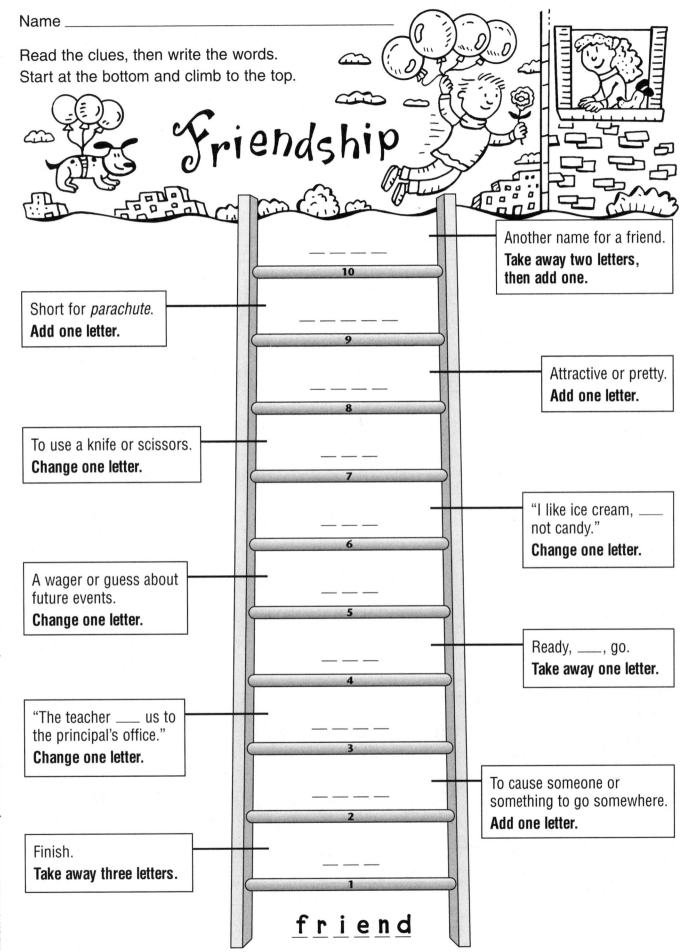

Friendship

Another name for a friend.
**Take away two letters,
then add one.**

10 _ _ _ _ _

Short for *parachute*.
Add one letter.

9 _ _ _ _ _

Attractive or pretty.
Add one letter.

8 _ _ _ _

To use a knife or scissors.
Change one letter.

7 _ _ _ _

"I like ice cream, ___
not candy."
Change one letter.

6 _ _ _

A wager or guess about
future events.
Change one letter.

5 _ _ _

Ready, ___, go.
Take away one letter.

4 _ _ _

"The teacher ___ us to
the principal's office."
Change one letter.

3 _ _ _ _

To cause someone or
something to go somewhere.
Add one letter.

2 _ _ _ _

Finish.
Take away three letters.

1

f r i e n d

Interactive Whiteboard Activities: Daily Word Ladders Grades 4–6 © 2012 Timothy V. Rasinski, Scholastic Teaching Resources

Name _____

Read the clues, then write the words.
Start at the bottom and climb to the top.

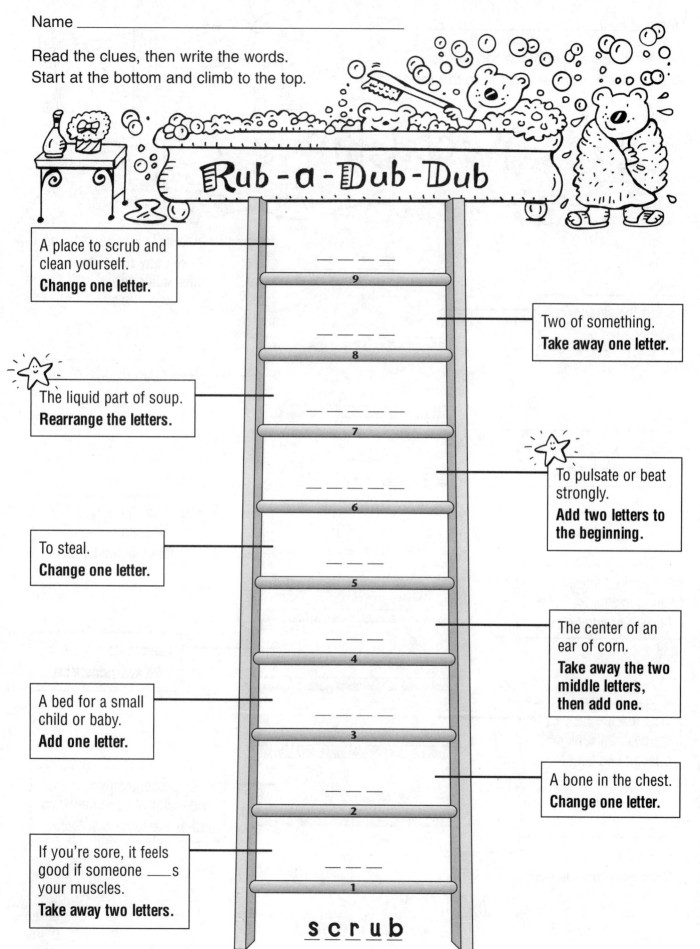

Rub-a-Dub-Dub

A place to scrub and clean yourself.
Change one letter.

Two of something.
Take away one letter.

The liquid part of soup.
Rearrange the letters.

To pulsate or beat strongly.
Add two letters to the beginning.

To steal.
Change one letter.

The center of an ear of corn.
Take away the two middle letters, then add one.

A bed for a small child or baby.
Add one letter.

A bone in the chest.
Change one letter.

If you're sore, it feels good if someone ___s your muscles.
Take away two letters.

9 — — — —
8 — — — —
7 — — — — —
6 — — — — —
5 — — —
4 — — —
3 — — — —
2 — — —
1 — — —

s c r u b

Interactive Whiteboard Activities: Daily Word Ladders Grades 4–6 © 2012 Timothy V. Rasinski, Scholastic Teaching Resources

Name _____

Read the clues, then write the words.
Start at the bottom and climb to the top.

Underwater

The gear divers use.
Add one letter.

10 _ _ _ _ _ _

A country that is an island
off the coast of Florida.
Add one letter.

9 _ _ _ _ _

A baby bear.
Change one letter.

8 _ _ _ _

Center part of a wheel.
Change the last letter.

7 _ _ _

Musical sound made
with the lips closed.
Change one letter.

6 _ _ _

A meat that comes
from a pig.
Take away two letters.

5 _ _ _

Short for *champion*.
Change one letter.

4 _ _ _ _ _

Short for *chimpanzee*.
Change one letter.

3 _ _ _ _ _

A musical instrument that
works when wind blows it.
**Take away the first letter,
then add two.**

2 _ _ _ _ _

A ten-cent coin.
Change one letter.

1 _ _ _ _

d i v e

Interactive Whiteboard Activities: Daily Word Ladders Grades 4–6 © 2012 Timothy V. Rasinski, Scholastic Teaching Resources

Name _____

Read the clues, then write the words.
Start at the bottom and climb to the top.

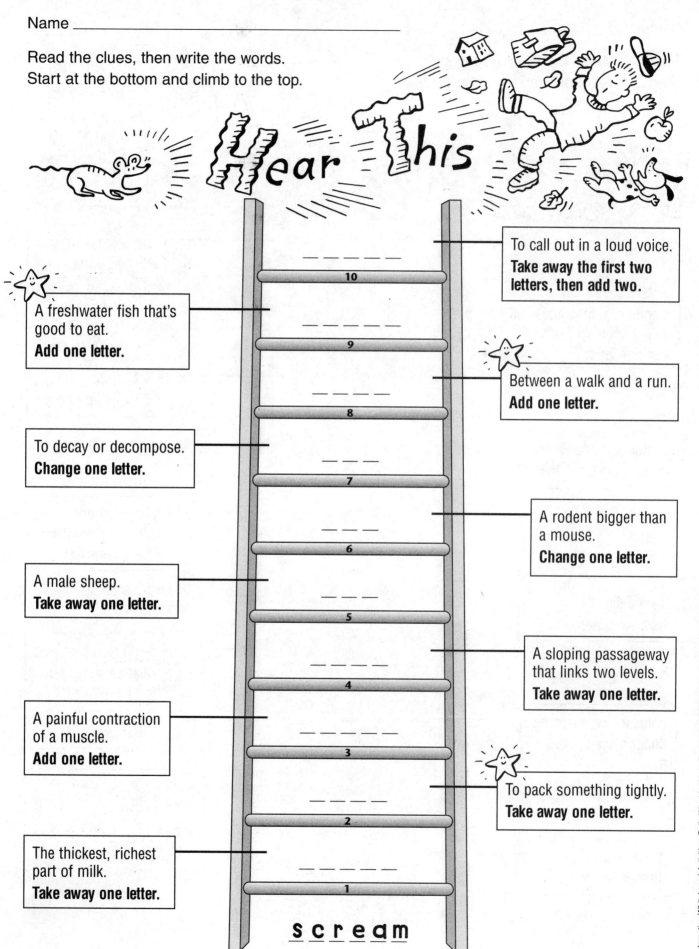

Hear This

To call out in a loud voice.
Take away the first two letters, then add two.

A freshwater fish that's good to eat.
Add one letter.

Between a walk and a run.
Add one letter.

To decay or decompose.
Change one letter.

A rodent bigger than a mouse.
Change one letter.

A male sheep.
Take away one letter.

A sloping passageway that links two levels.
Take away one letter.

A painful contraction of a muscle.
Add one letter.

To pack something tightly.
Take away one letter.

The thickest, richest part of milk.
Take away one letter.

10
9
8
7
6
5
4
3
2
1

s c r e a m

Interactive Whiteboard Activities: *Daily Word Ladders Grades 4–6* © 2012 Timothy V. Rasinski, Scholastic Teaching Resources

Name _____

Read the clues, then write the words.
Start at the bottom and climb to the top.

Brainy Birds

Another bird of prey.
Change one letter.

11 _ _ _ _ _

Another word for *cough*.
Change one letter.

10 _ _ _ _ _

Short for *Henry*.
Change one letter.

9 _ _ _ _ _

This has five fingers.
Take away two letters.

8 _ _ _ _

A part of an object that you hold.
Change one letter.

7 _ _ _ _ _ _

Something made of wax that you can light.
Change the first two letters.

6 _ _ _ _ _ _

A package or a group of related things.
Change one letter.

5 _ _ _ _ _

To mishandle or botch things up.
Add one letter after the *u*.

4 _ _ _ _ _

A kind of horn or trumpet used in the army.
Change the first vowel, then rearrange the letters.

3 _ _ _ _

A round, chewy bread with a hole in the middle.
Take away a vowel, then rearrange the letters.

2 _ _ _ _ _

A small hound dog with long ears.
Add one letter.

1 _ _ _ _ _

e a g l e

Name _____

Read the clues, then write the words.
Start at the bottom and climb to the top.

Itchy (and) Scratchy

What you do to an itch.
Add two letters.

⎯ ⎯ ⎯ ⎯ ⎯ ⎯ ⎯
11

⎯ ⎯ ⎯ ⎯ ⎯ ⎯
10

To grab a ball as it flies
through the air.
Change one letter.

To cover a hole in clothes.
Change one letter.

⎯ ⎯ ⎯ ⎯ ⎯ ⎯
9

⎯ ⎯ ⎯ ⎯ ⎯
8

To throw a baseball
to a batter.
Change one letter.

What cowboys do to horses
to keep them in one place.
Change the vowel.

⎯ ⎯ ⎯ ⎯ ⎯
7

⎯ ⎯ ⎯ ⎯ ⎯
6

A pen to keep rabbits in.
Replace the *n*.

A guess.
Change the first letter.

⎯ ⎯ ⎯ ⎯ ⎯
5

⎯ ⎯ ⎯ ⎯ ⎯
4

Noontime meal.
Change one letter.

Boxers do this.
Change one letter.

⎯ ⎯ ⎯ ⎯ ⎯
3

⎯ ⎯ ⎯ ⎯ ⎯
2

To hurt by squeezing
the skin.
Add one letter.

Twelve of these make a foot.
Change one letter.

⎯ ⎯ ⎯ ⎯
1

i t c h

Interactive Whiteboard Activities: Daily Word Ladders Grades 4–6 © 2012 Timothy V. Rasinski, Scholastic Teaching Resources

Name _____

Read the clues, then write the words.
Start at the bottom and climb to the top.

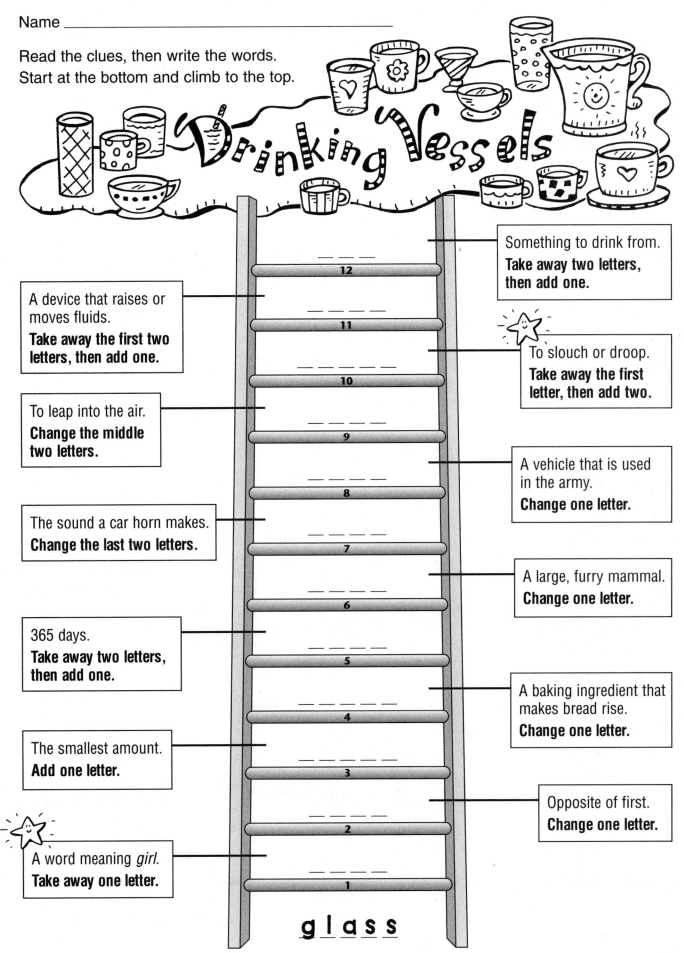

Drinking Vessels

Something to drink from.
Take away two letters, then add one.

A device that raises or moves fluids.
Take away the first two letters, then add one.

To slouch or droop.
Take away the first letter, then add two.

To leap into the air.
Change the middle two letters.

A vehicle that is used in the army.
Change one letter.

The sound a car horn makes.
Change the last two letters.

A large, furry mammal.
Change one letter.

365 days.
Take away two letters, then add one.

A baking ingredient that makes bread rise.
Change one letter.

The smallest amount.
Add one letter.

Opposite of first.
Change one letter.

A word meaning *girl*.
Take away one letter.

12
11
10
9
8
7
6
5
4
3
2
1

g l a s s

Interactive Whiteboard Activities: Daily Word Ladders Grades 4–6 © 2012 Timothy V. Rasinski, Scholastic Teaching Resources

Name _____

Read the clues, then write the words.
Start at the bottom and climb to the top.

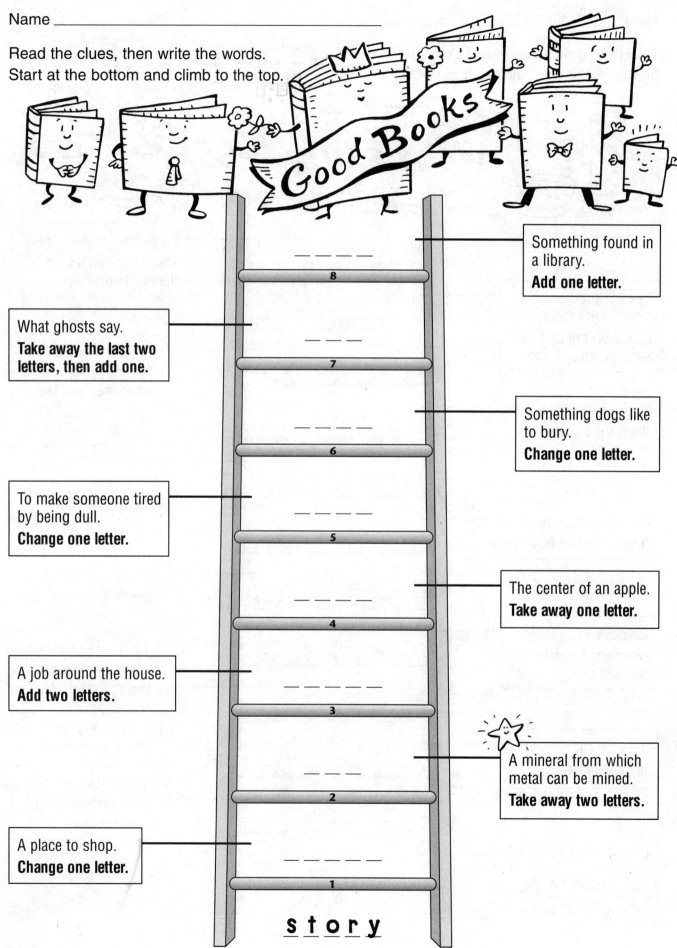

Good Books

Something found in a library.
Add one letter.

8 _ _ _ _ _

What ghosts say.
Take away the last two letters, then add one.

7 _ _ _

Something dogs like to bury.
Change one letter.

6 _ _ _ _ _

To make someone tired by being dull.
Change one letter.

5 _ _ _ _

The center of an apple.
Take away one letter.

4 _ _ _ _ _

A job around the house.
Add two letters.

3 _ _ _ _ _ _

A mineral from which metal can be mined.
Take away two letters.

2 _ _ _

A place to shop.
Change one letter.

1 _ _ _ _ _

s t o r y

68

Interactive Whiteboard Activities: Daily Word Ladders Grades 4–6 © 2012 Timothy V. Rasinski, Scholastic Teaching Resources

Name _____

Read the clues, then write the words.
Start at the bottom and climb to the top.

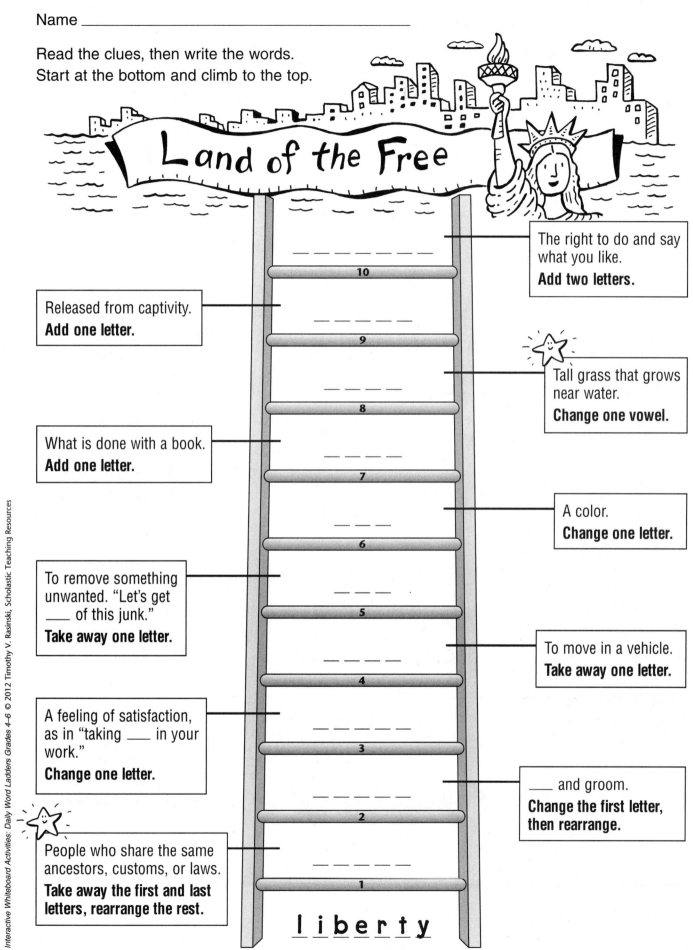

Land of the Free

The right to do and say what you like.
Add two letters.

Released from captivity.
Add one letter.

Tall grass that grows near water.
Change one vowel.

What is done with a book.
Add one letter.

A color.
Change one letter.

To remove something unwanted. "Let's get ___ of this junk."
Take away one letter.

To move in a vehicle.
Take away one letter.

A feeling of satisfaction, as in "taking ___ in your work."
Change one letter.

___ and groom.
Change the first letter, then rearrange.

People who share the same ancestors, customs, or laws.
Take away the first and last letters, rearrange the rest.

10

9

8

7

6

5

4

3

2

1

l i b e r t y

Name _____

Read the clues, then write the words.
Start at the bottom and climb to the top.

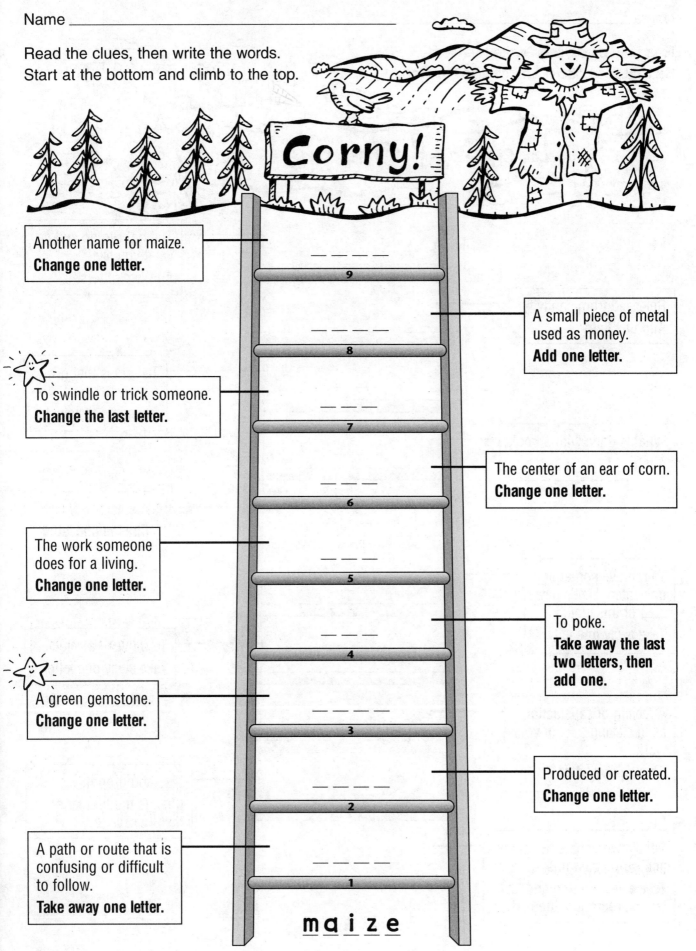

Corny!

Another name for maize.
Change one letter.

_ _ _ _ _
9

A small piece of metal used as money.
Add one letter.

_ _ _ _ _
8

To swindle or trick someone.
Change the last letter.

_ _ _
7

The center of an ear of corn.
Change one letter.

_ _ _
6

The work someone does for a living.
Change one letter.

_ _ _ _
5

To poke.
Take away the last two letters, then add one.

_ _ _
4

A green gemstone.
Change one letter.

_ _ _ _
3

Produced or created.
Change one letter.

_ _ _ _ _
2

A path or route that is confusing or difficult to follow.
Take away one letter.

_ _ _ _ _
1

m a i z e

Interactive Whiteboard Activities: Daily Word Ladders Grades 4–6 © 2012 Timothy V. Rasinski, Scholastic Teaching Resources

Name _____

Read the clues, then write the words.
Start at the bottom and climb to the top.

School Days

Where you live.
Change one letter.

_ _ _ _ _

9

An opening in something.
Change one letter.

_ _ _ _

8

To carry or support something.
Change one letter.

_ _ _ _

7

Exchanged something for money.
Take away one letter.

_ _ _ _

6

To criticize.
Add one letter.

_ _ _ _ _

5

Opposite of hot.
Change one letter.

_ _ _ _

4

A popular soft drink flavor.
Rearrange the letters.

_ _ _ _

3

A black rock-like substance that can be burned.
Change one letter.

_ _ _ _

2

Slightly cold.
Take away two letters.

_ _ _ _

1

s c h o o l

Name _____

Read the clues, then write the words.
Start at the bottom and climb to the top.

Jobs for Grownups

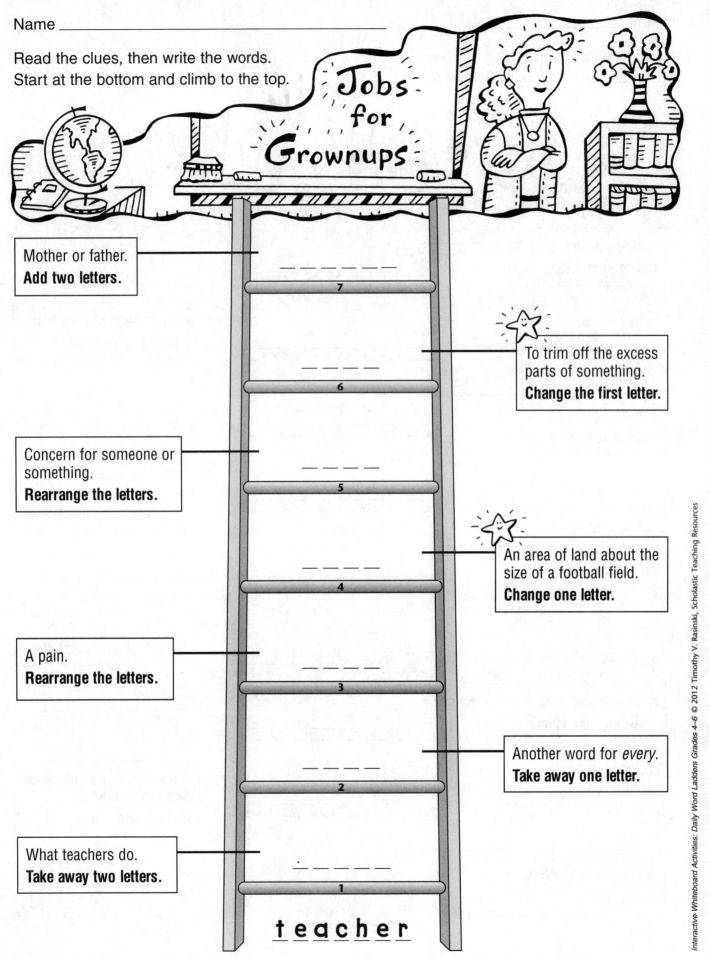

Mother or father.
Add two letters.

7
_ _ _ _ _ _

To trim off the excess parts of something.
Change the first letter.

6
_ _ _ _ _

Concern for someone or something.
Rearrange the letters.

5
_ _ _ _ _

An area of land about the size of a football field.
Change one letter.

4
_ _ _ _ _

A pain.
Rearrange the letters.

3
_ _ _ _ _

Another word for *every*.
Take away one letter.

2
_ _ _ _

What teachers do.
Take away two letters.

1
._ _ _ _ _

t e a c h e r

Interactive Whiteboard Activities: Daily Word Ladders Grades 4–6 © 2012 Timothy V. Rasinski, Scholastic Teaching Resources

Name _____

Read the clues, then write the words.
Start at the bottom and climb to the top.

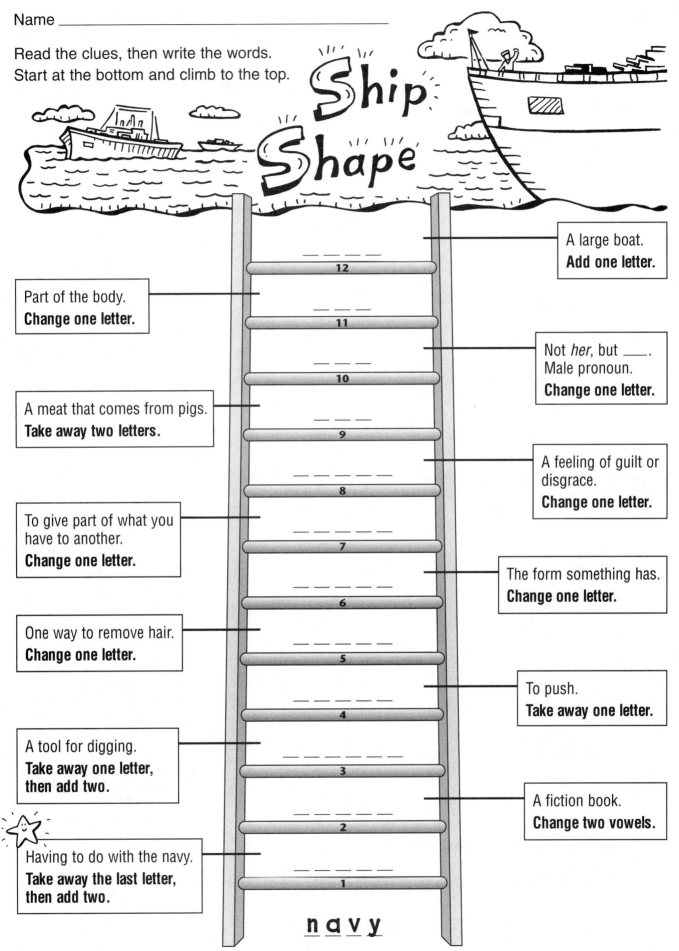

Ship Shape

A large boat.
Add one letter.

Part of the body.
Change one letter.

Not *her*, but ___.
Male pronoun.
Change one letter.

A meat that comes from pigs.
Take away two letters.

A feeling of guilt or disgrace.
Change one letter.

To give part of what you have to another.
Change one letter.

The form something has.
Change one letter.

One way to remove hair.
Change one letter.

To push.
Take away one letter.

A tool for digging.
Take away one letter, then add two.

A fiction book.
Change two vowels.

Having to do with the navy.
Take away the last letter, then add two.

12

11

10

9

8

7

6

5

4

3

2

1

n a v y

Interactive Whiteboard Activities: Daily Word Ladders Grades 4–6 © 2012 Timothy V. Rasinski, Scholastic Teaching Resources

Name _____

Read the clues, then write the words.
Start at the bottom and climb to the top.

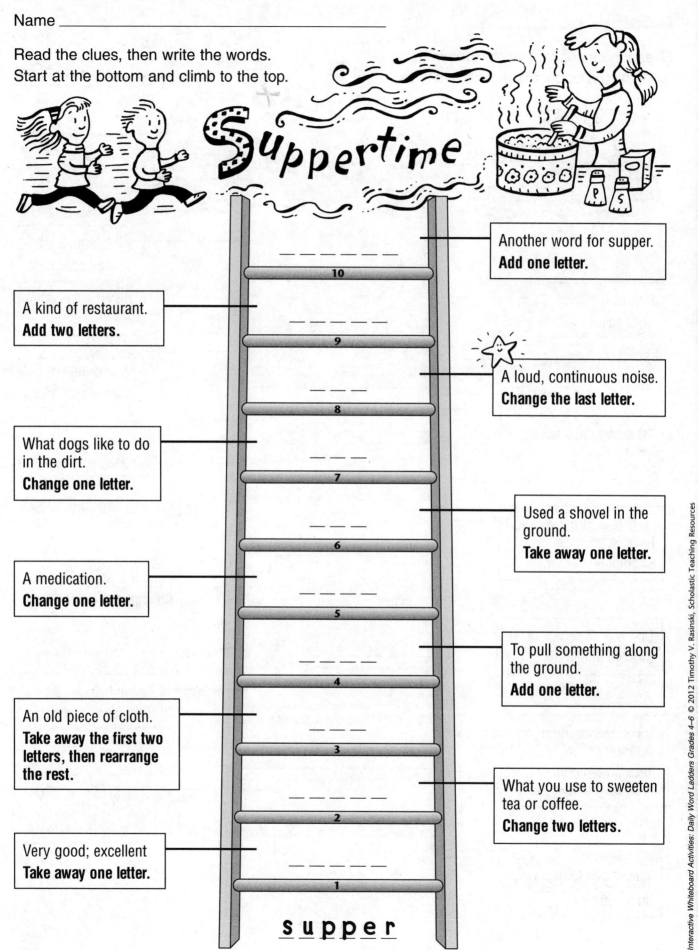

Suppertime

Another word for supper.
Add one letter.

10 _ _ _ _ _ _ _

A kind of restaurant.
Add two letters.

9 _ _ _ _ _ _

A loud, continuous noise.
Change the last letter.

8 _ _ _

What dogs like to do in the dirt.
Change one letter.

7 _ _ _ _

Used a shovel in the ground.
Take away one letter.

6 _ _ _

A medication.
Change one letter.

5 _ _ _ _ _

To pull something along the ground.
Add one letter.

4 _ _ _ _

An old piece of cloth.
Take away the first two letters, then rearrange the rest.

3 _ _ _

What you use to sweeten tea or coffee.
Change two letters.

2 _ _ _ _ _

Very good; excellent
Take away one letter.

1 _ _ _ _ _

s u p p e r

Interactive Whiteboard Activities: Daily Word Ladders Grades 4–6 © 2012 Timothy V. Rasinski, Scholastic Teaching Resources

Name _____

Read the clues, then write the words.
Start at the bottom and climb to the top.

Just a Spoonful

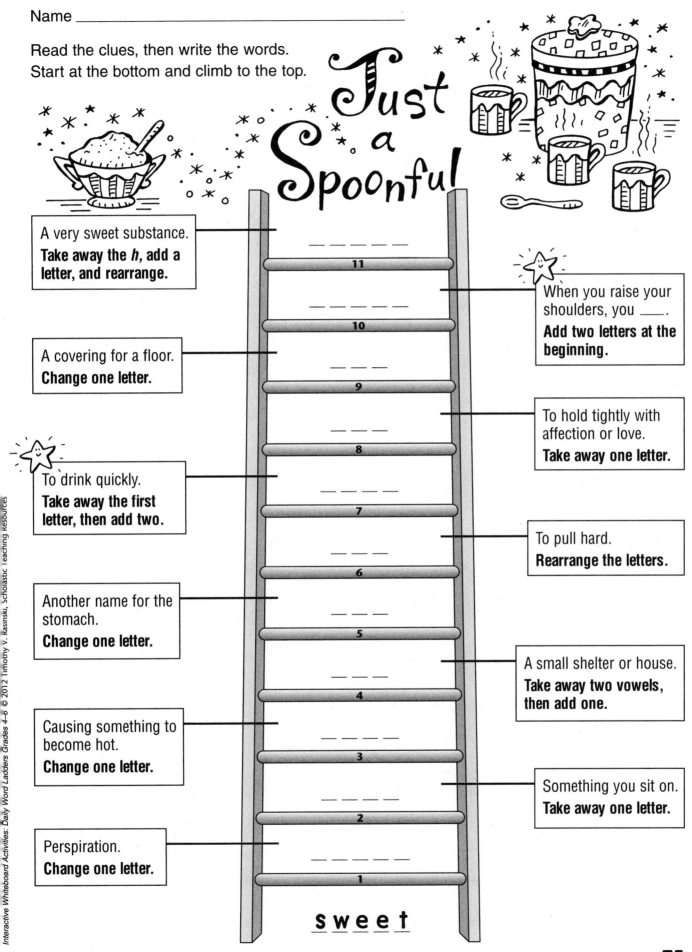

A very sweet substance.
Take away the *h*, add a letter, and rearrange.

When you raise your shoulders, you ____.
Add two letters at the beginning.

A covering for a floor.
Change one letter.

To hold tightly with affection or love.
Take away one letter.

To drink quickly.
Take away the first letter, then add two.

To pull hard.
Rearrange the letters.

Another name for the stomach.
Change one letter.

A small shelter or house.
Take away two vowels, then add one.

Causing something to become hot.
Change one letter.

Something you sit on.
Take away one letter.

Perspiration.
Change one letter.

11
10
9
8
7
6
5
4
3
2
1

s w e e t

Name _____

Read the clues, then write the words.
Start at the bottom and climb to the top.

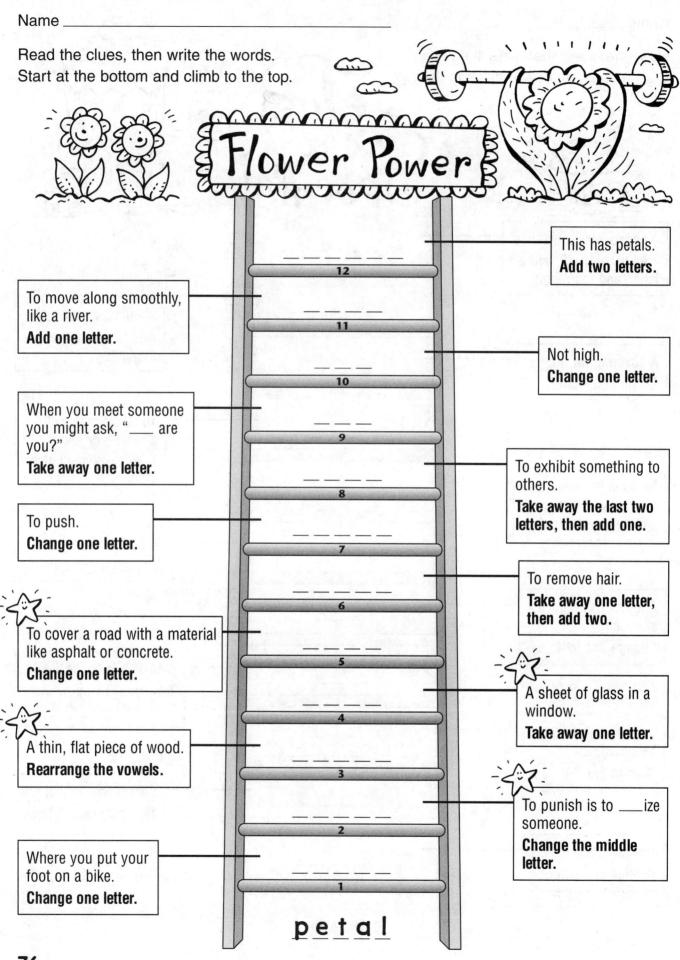

Flower Power

This has petals.
Add two letters.

To move along smoothly, like a river.
Add one letter.

Not high.
Change one letter.

When you meet someone you might ask, "___ are you?"
Take away one letter.

To exhibit something to others.
Take away the last two letters, then add one.

To push.
Change one letter.

To remove hair.
Take away one letter, then add two.

To cover a road with a material like asphalt or concrete.
Change one letter.

A sheet of glass in a window.
Take away one letter.

A thin, flat piece of wood.
Rearrange the vowels.

To punish is to ___ize someone.
Change the middle letter.

Where you put your foot on a bike.
Change one letter.

p e t a l

Interactive Whiteboard Activities: Daily Word Ladders Grades 4–6 © 2012 Timothy V. Rasinski, Scholastic Teaching Resources

Name _____

Read the clues, then write the words.
Start at the bottom and climb to the top.

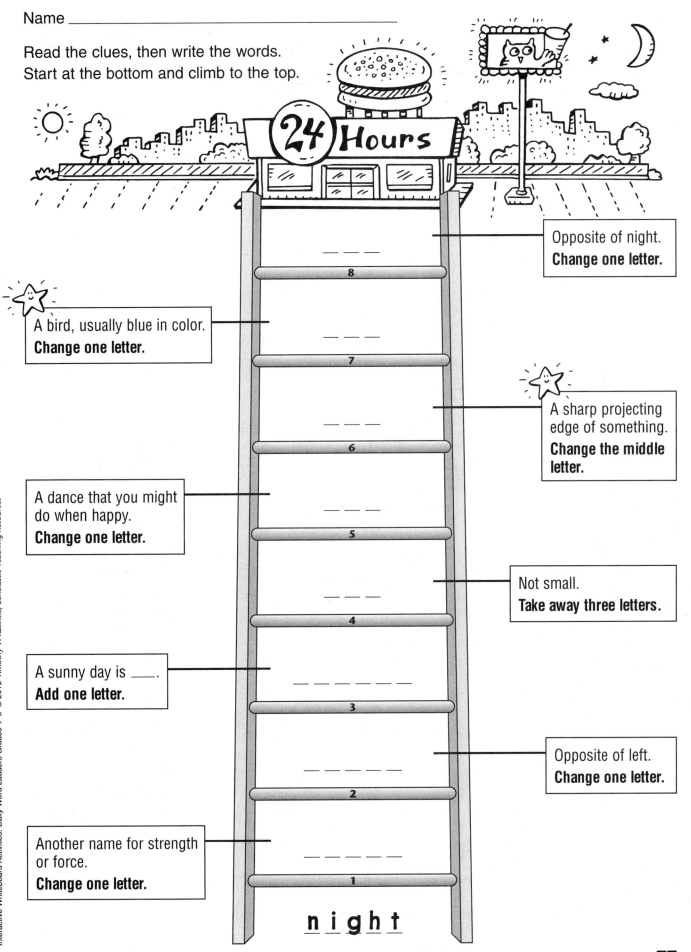

24 Hours

Opposite of night.
Change one letter.

A bird, usually blue in color.
Change one letter.

A sharp projecting edge of something.
Change the middle letter.

A dance that you might do when happy.
Change one letter.

Not small.
Take away three letters.

A sunny day is ___.
Add one letter.

Opposite of left.
Change one letter.

Another name for strength or force.
Change one letter.

8 ___ ___ ___

7 ___ ___ ___

6 ___ ___ ___

5 ___ ___ ___

4 ___ ___ ___

3 ___ ___ ___ ___ ___ ___

2 ___ ___ ___ ___ ___

1 ___ ___ ___ ___ ___

n i g h t

Name _____

Read the clues, then write the words.
Start at the bottom and climb to the top.

Colts belong to this family of animals.
Change one letter.

You use dots and dashes in ___ Code.
Add one letter.

An additional or greater amount of something.
Change one letter.

A female horse.
Change one letter.

A word for market or store.
Change one letter.

A long pole coming from the center of the deck of a ship.
Change the vowel.

The opposite of least.
Change one letter.

The person who gives a party.
Change one letter.

The price of something.
Change one letter.

9
8
7
6
5
4
3
2
1

c o l t

Interactive Whiteboard Activities: Daily Word Ladders Grades 4–6 © 2012 Timothy V. Rasinski, Scholastic Teaching Resources

Name _____

Read the clues, then write the words.
Start at the bottom and climb to the top.

Voting Booth

8 _ _ _ _ _

This is often done by casting a ballot.
Change one letter.

A short, informal letter.
Change one letter.

7 _ _ _ _

To carry.
Add one letter.

6 _ _ _ _

A young child.
Change one letter.

5 _ _ _

A large quantity of something.
Change one letter.

4 _ _ _

To permit. "I hope mom ____s us go."
Take away three letters.

3 _ _ _

A kind of dance.
Add two letters.

2 _ _ _ _ _

A round object.
Take away two letters.

1 _ _ _ _

b a l l o t

Interactive Whiteboard Activities: Daily Word Ladders Grades 4–6 © 2012 Timothy V. Rasinski, Scholastic Teaching Resources

Name _____

Read the clues, then write the words.
Start at the bottom and climb to the top.

Sailing

A craft for traveling on water.
Change one letter.

You wear this in winter.
Add one letter.

A pet animal related to tigers and lions.
Change one letter.

To touch or hit lightly.
Change one letter.

A friend.
Take away one letter.

A kind of tree found in tropical places.
Change one letter.

A state of tranquillity; not bothered by anything.
Rearrange the letters.

A shelled animal that lives at the bottom of the sea.
Take away one letter.

To assert something.
"He ___s he didn't do it."
Add two letters.

To shoot, hit, or throw in a particular direction.
Change one letter.

To be ill.
Take away two letters.

A slow-moving animal.
Add one letter.

12 _ _ _ _

11 _ _ _ _

10 _ _ _ _

9 _ _ _

8 _ _ _ _

7 _ _ _ _ _

6 _ _ _ _ _

5 _ _ _ _ _

4 _ _ _ _ _

3 _ _ _ _

2 _ _ _

1 _ _ _ _

s a i l

Interactive Whiteboard Activities: Daily Word Ladders Grades 4–6 © 2012 Timothy V. Rasinski, Scholastic Teaching Resources

Name _____

Read the clues, then write the words.
Start at the bottom and climb to the top.

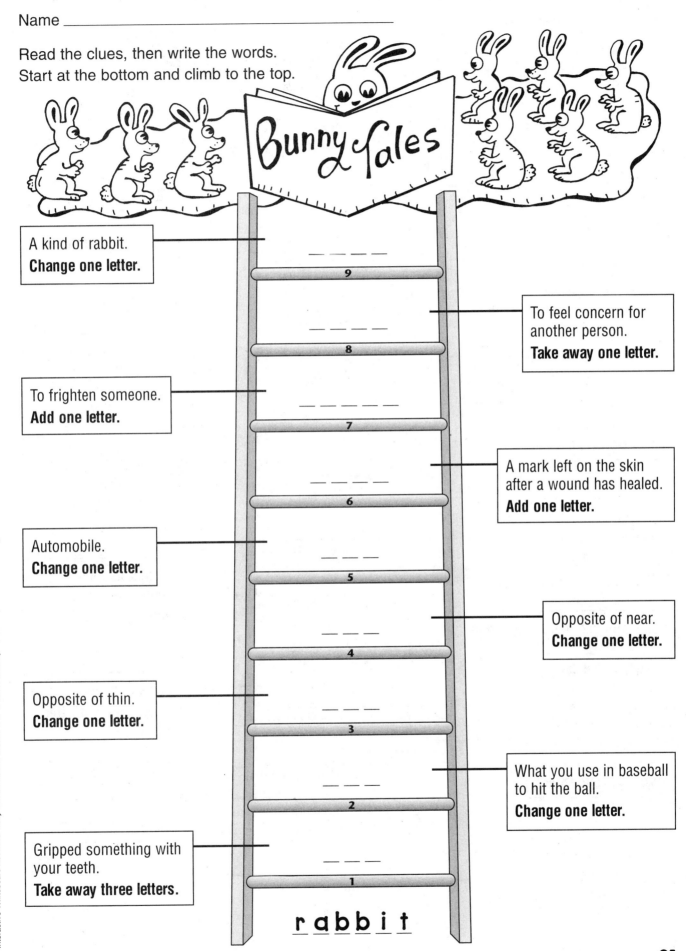

Bunny Tales

A kind of rabbit.
Change one letter.

_ _ _ _ _   9

To feel concern for another person.
Take away one letter.

_ _ _ _ _   8

To frighten someone.
Add one letter.

_ _ _ _ _   7

A mark left on the skin after a wound has healed.
Add one letter.

_ _ _ _   6

Automobile.
Change one letter.

_ _ _ _   5

Opposite of near.
Change one letter.

_ _ _ _   4

Opposite of thin.
Change one letter.

_ _ _ _   3

What you use in baseball to hit the ball.
Change one letter.

_ _ _   2

Gripped something with your teeth.
Take away three letters.

_ _ _   1

r a b b i t

Name _____

Read the clues, then write the words.
Start at the bottom and climb to the top. **Good**

Hare Day

Another name for a hare.
Add two letters.

_ _ _ _ _
12

A piece of bread, usually in the form of a round roll.
Change one letter.

_ _ _ _
11

On the other hand. "I like school, ___ recess should be longer."
Change one letter.

_ _ _ _
10

A winged mammal that usually flies at night.
Change one letter.

_ _ _
9

A long, flat block of something hard, like a chocolate ___.
Take away one letter.

_ _ _ _
8

Uncovered; without clothing.
Change one letter.

_ _ _ _ _
7

Another name for a poet.
Change the first letter.

_ _ _ _ _
6

You might get one of these in the mail on your birthday.
Change one letter.

_ _ _ _ _
5

A type of fish.
Change the first letter.

_ _ _ _ _
4

A stringed musical instrument.
Take away one letter.

_ _ _ _ _
3

Pointed, not dull.
Change one letter.

_ _ _ _ _ _
2

To give some of what you have to others.
Add one letter.

_ _ _ _ _
1

h a r e

Interactive Whiteboard Activities: Daily Word Ladders Grades 4–6 © 2012 Timothy V. Rasinski, Scholastic Teaching Resources

Name _____

Read the clues, then write the words.
Start at the bottom and climb to the top.

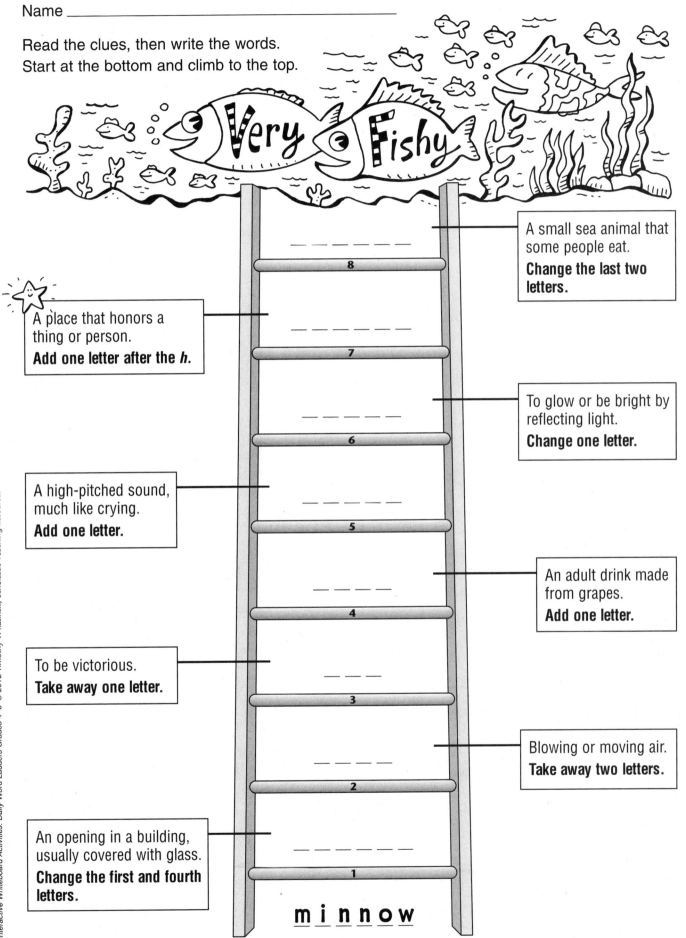

Very Fishy

A small sea animal that some people eat.
Change the last two letters.

A place that honors a thing or person.
Add one letter after the _h_.

To glow or be bright by reflecting light.
Change one letter.

A high-pitched sound, much like crying.
Add one letter.

An adult drink made from grapes.
Add one letter.

To be victorious.
Take away one letter.

Blowing or moving air.
Take away two letters.

An opening in a building, usually covered with glass.
Change the first and fourth letters.

8

7

6

5

4

3

2

1

m i n n o w

Interactive Whiteboard Activities: Daily Word Ladders Grades 4–6 © 2012 Timothy V. Rasinski, Scholastic Teaching Resources

Name _____

Read the clues, then write the words.
Start at the bottom and climb to the top.

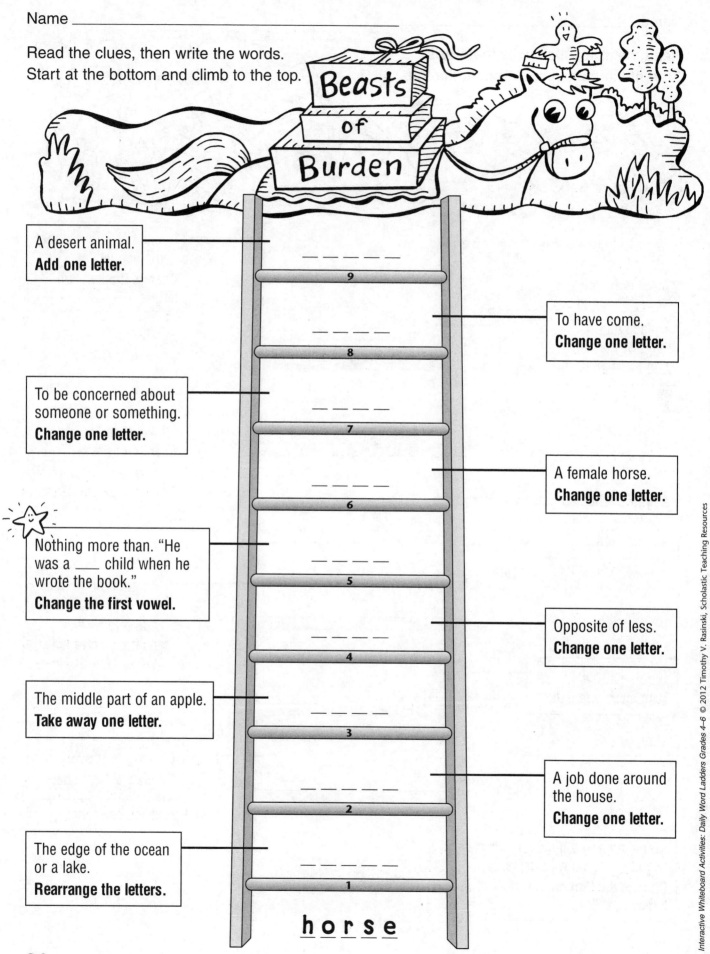

Beasts of Burden

A desert animal.
Add one letter.

_ _ _ _ _
9

To have come.
Change one letter.

_ _ _ _ _
8

To be concerned about
someone or something.
Change one letter.

_ _ _ _ _
7

A female horse.
Change one letter.

_ _ _ _ _
6

Nothing more than. "He
was a ___ child when he
wrote the book."
Change the first vowel.

_ _ _ _ _
5

Opposite of less.
Change one letter.

_ _ _ _ _
4

The middle part of an apple.
Take away one letter.

_ _ _ _ _
3

A job done around
the house.
Change one letter.

_ _ _ _ _
2

The edge of the ocean
or a lake.
Rearrange the letters.

_ _ _ _ _
1

h o r s e

84

Interactive Whiteboard Activities: Daily Word Ladders Grades 4–6 © 2012 Timothy V. Rasinski, Scholastic Teaching Resources

Name _____

Read the clues, then write the words.
Start at the bottom and climb to the top.

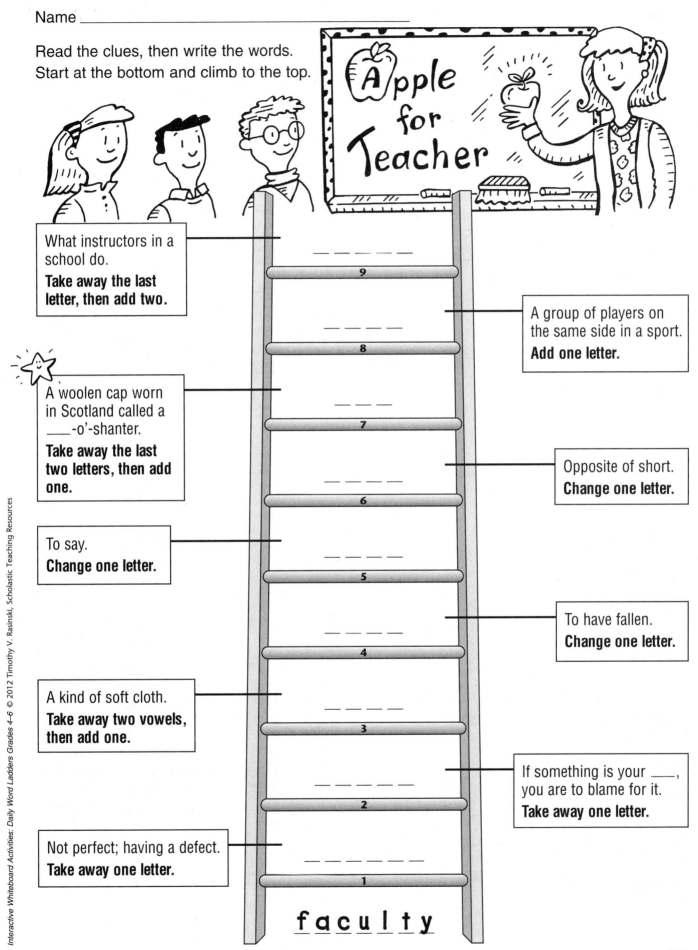

What instructors in a school do.
Take away the last letter, then add two.

A woolen cap worn in Scotland called a ___-o'-shanter.
Take away the last two letters, then add one.

To say.
Change one letter.

A kind of soft cloth.
Take away two vowels, then add one.

Not perfect; having a defect.
Take away one letter.

A group of players on the same side in a sport.
Add one letter.

Opposite of short.
Change one letter.

To have fallen.
Change one letter.

If something is your ___, you are to blame for it.
Take away one letter.

9

8

7

6

5

4

3

2

1

f a c u l t y

Interactive Whiteboard Activities: Daily Word Ladders Grades 4–6 © 2012 Timothy V. Rasinski, Scholastic Teaching Resources

Name _____

Read the clues, then write the words.
Start at the bottom and climb to the top.

Art Smart!

A place to display works of art.
Add one letter.

— — — — — — — —   **11**

The kitchen and cooking area of a ship or airplane.
Add one letter to the beginning.

— — — — — —   **10**

A narrow street with access to the rear of buildings.
Add two letters.

— — — — —   **9**

Everyone and everything.
Take away one letter.

— — —   **8**

An enclosed shopping center.
Change one letter.

— — — —   **7**

Opposite of short.
Change one letter.

— — — —   **6**

To speak.
Change one letter.

— — — — —   **5**

A little nail for hanging things, as on a bulletin board.
Change one letter.

— — — —   **4**

What you do with a suitcase.
Change one letter.

— — — —   **3**

A place for recreation.
Change one letter.

— — — —   **2**

Some, but not all, of something.
Add one letter.

— — — —   **1**

a r t

86

Interactive Whiteboard Activities: Daily Word Ladders Grades 4–6 © 2012 Timothy V. Rasinski, Scholastic Teaching Resources

Name _____

Read the clues, then write the words.
Start at the bottom and climb to the top.

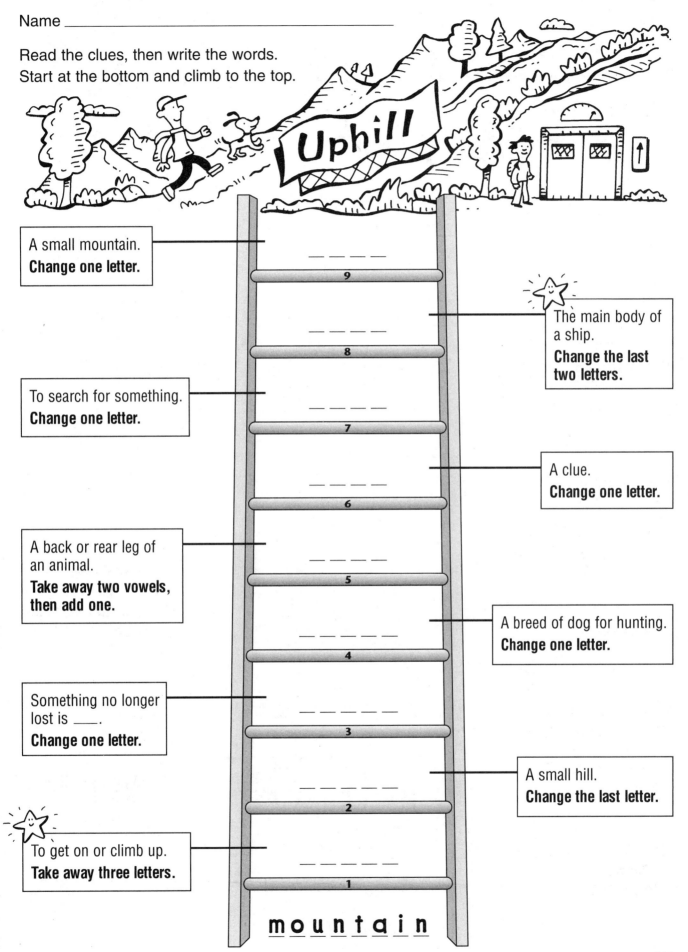

A small mountain.
Change one letter.

A small mountain. — 9

The main body of a ship.
Change the last two letters. — 8

To search for something.
Change one letter. — 7

A clue.
Change one letter. — 6

A back or rear leg of an animal.
Take away two vowels, then add one. — 5

A breed of dog for hunting.
Change one letter. — 4

Something no longer lost is ___.
Change one letter. — 3

A small hill.
Change the last letter. — 2

To get on or climb up.
Take away three letters. — 1

m o u n t a i n

Interactive Whiteboard Activities: Daily Word Ladders Grades 4–6 © 2012 Timothy V. Rasinski, Scholastic Teaching Resources

Name _____

Read the clues, then write the words.
Start at the bottom and climb to the top.

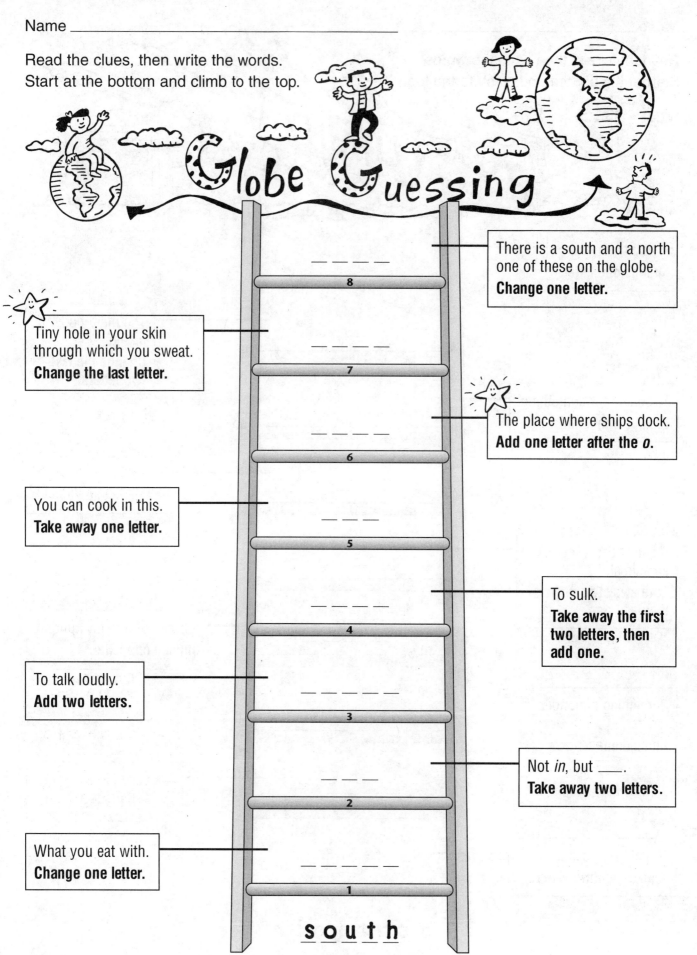

Globe Guessing

There is a south and a north
one of these on the globe.
Change one letter.

8 ___ ___ ___ ___

Tiny hole in your skin
through which you sweat.
Change the last letter.

7 ___ ___ ___ ___

The place where ships dock.
Add one letter after the *o*.

6 ___ ___ ___ ___

You can cook in this.
Take away one letter.

5 ___ ___ ___

To sulk.
**Take away the first
two letters, then
add one.**

4 ___ ___ ___ ___

To talk loudly.
Add two letters.

3 ___ ___ ___ ___ ___

Not *in*, but ___.
Take away two letters.

2 ___ ___ ___

What you eat with.
Change one letter.

1 ___ ___ ___ ___ ___

s o u t h

88

Interactive Whiteboard Activities: Daily Word Ladders Grades 4–6 © 2012 Timothy V. Rasinski, Scholastic Teaching Resources

Name _____

Read the clues, then write the words.
Start at the bottom and climb to the top.

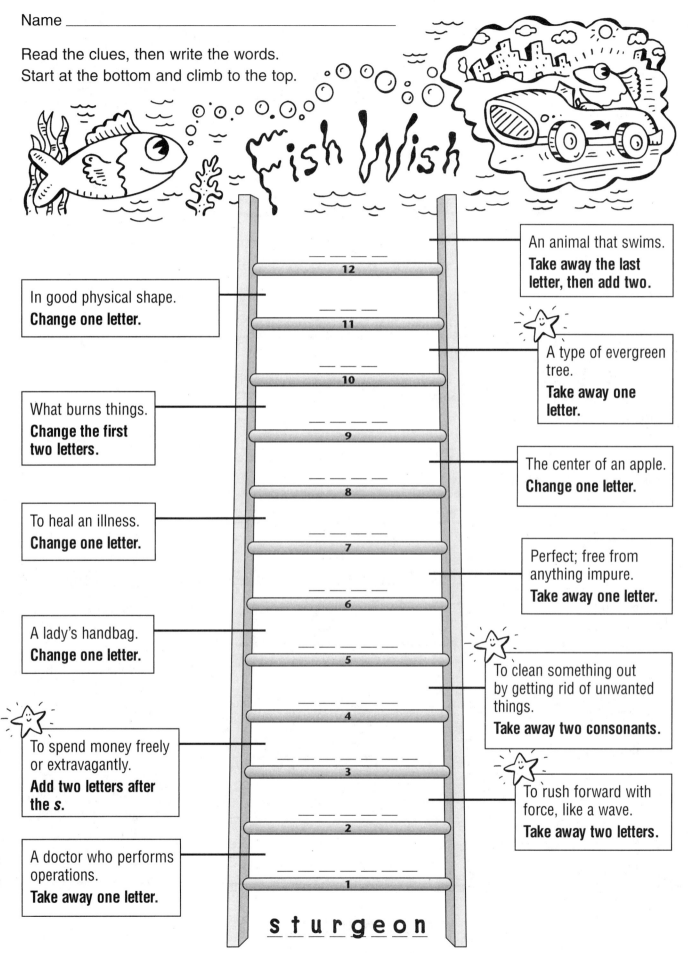

Fish Wish

An animal that swims.
Take away the last letter, then add two.

In good physical shape.
Change one letter.

A type of evergreen tree.
Take away one letter.

What burns things.
Change the first two letters.

The center of an apple.
Change one letter.

To heal an illness.
Change one letter.

Perfect; free from anything impure.
Take away one letter.

A lady's handbag.
Change one letter.

To clean something out by getting rid of unwanted things.
Take away two consonants.

To spend money freely or extravagantly.
Add two letters after the s.

To rush forward with force, like a wave.
Take away two letters.

A doctor who performs operations.
Take away one letter.

12
11
10
9
8
7
6
5
4
3
2
1

s t u r g e o n

Name _____

Read the clues, then write the words.
Start at the bottom and climb to the top.

From the Ground Up

To build again.
Add two letters.

– – – – – – – –
11

– – – – – –
10

To make something by putting parts together.
Add two letters after the *u*.

A small shoot that will grow into a leaf or flower.
Take away the last two letters, then add one.

– – –
9

– – – –
8

A shrub.
Take away one letter.

You use this on your hair.
Change the first and last letters.

– – – – – –
7

– – – – –
6

To believe in someone or something.
Take away three letters.

When you don't trust someone, you ___ him.
Change two letters after the *r*.

– – – – – – – –
5

– – – – – – –
4

To weaken someone's concentration.
Change two vowels.

To tear something down.
Change the first two letters.

– – – – – – –
3

– – – – – – –
2

To teach something.
Take away the first two letters, then add one.

To build something.
Take away two letters.

– – – – – – – –
1

r e c o n s t r u c t

Interactive Whiteboard Activities: Daily Word Ladders Grades 4–6 © 2012 Timothy V. Rasinski, Scholastic Teaching Resources

Name _____

Read the clues, then write the words.
Start at the bottom and climb to the top.

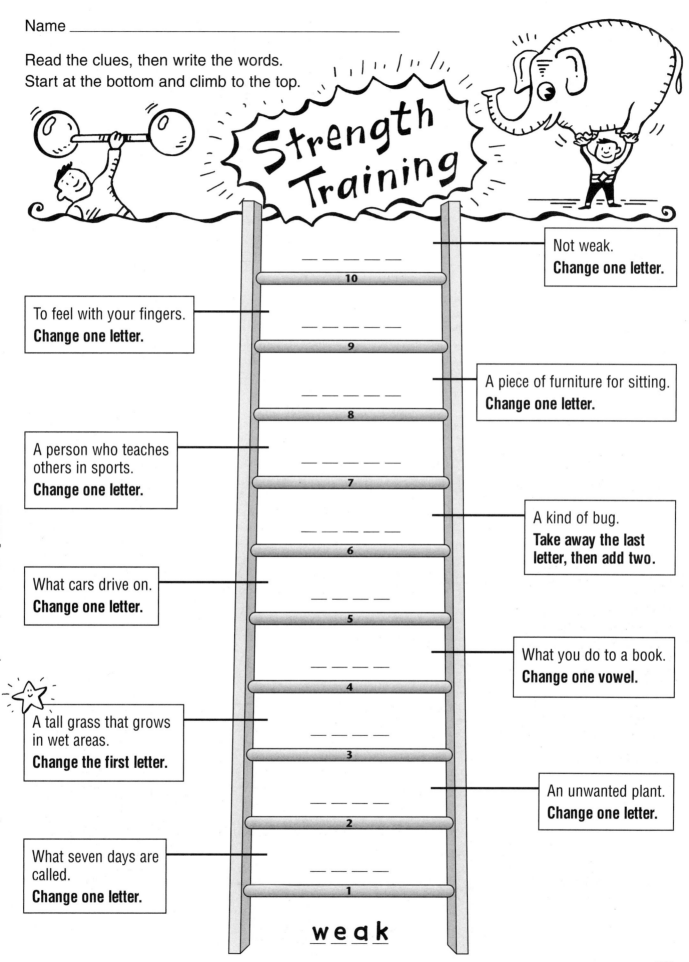

Strength Training

Not weak.
Change one letter.

To feel with your fingers.
Change one letter.

A piece of furniture for sitting.
Change one letter.

A person who teaches others in sports.
Change one letter.

A kind of bug.
Take away the last letter, then add two.

What cars drive on.
Change one letter.

What you do to a book.
Change one vowel.

A tall grass that grows in wet areas.
Change the first letter.

An unwanted plant.
Change one letter.

What seven days are called.
Change one letter.

10
9
8
7
6
5
4
3
2
1

w e a k

Interactive Whiteboard Activities: Daily Word Ladders Grades 4–6 © 2012 Timothy V. Rasinski, Scholastic Teaching Resources

Name _____

Read the clues, then write the words.
Start at the bottom and climb to the top.

Getting the Message

A kind of written message.
Add one letter.

10 _ _ _ _ _

Do ___ go where it is dangerous.
Change one letter.

9 _ _ _

It hangs from a basketball rim.
Take away one letter.

8 _ _ _

The home for a bird.
Change one letter.

7 _ _ _ _

Direction in which the sun sets.
Take away two letters, then add one.

6 _ _ _ _

Part of the body at the end of the arm.
Take away one letter, then add two.

5 _ _ _ _ _

A light rain.
Change one letter.

4 _ _ _ _

To feel bad that someone is absent.
Change one letter.

3 _ _ _ _

A number of people or things together.
Take away three letters.

2 _ _ _ _

To rub the muscles.
Change one letter.

1 _ _ _ _ _ _ _

m e s s a g e

92

Interactive Whiteboard Activities: Daily Word Ladders Grades 4–6 © 2012 Timothy V. Rasinski, Scholastic Teaching Resources

Name _____

Read the clues, then write the words.
Start at the bottom and climb to the top.

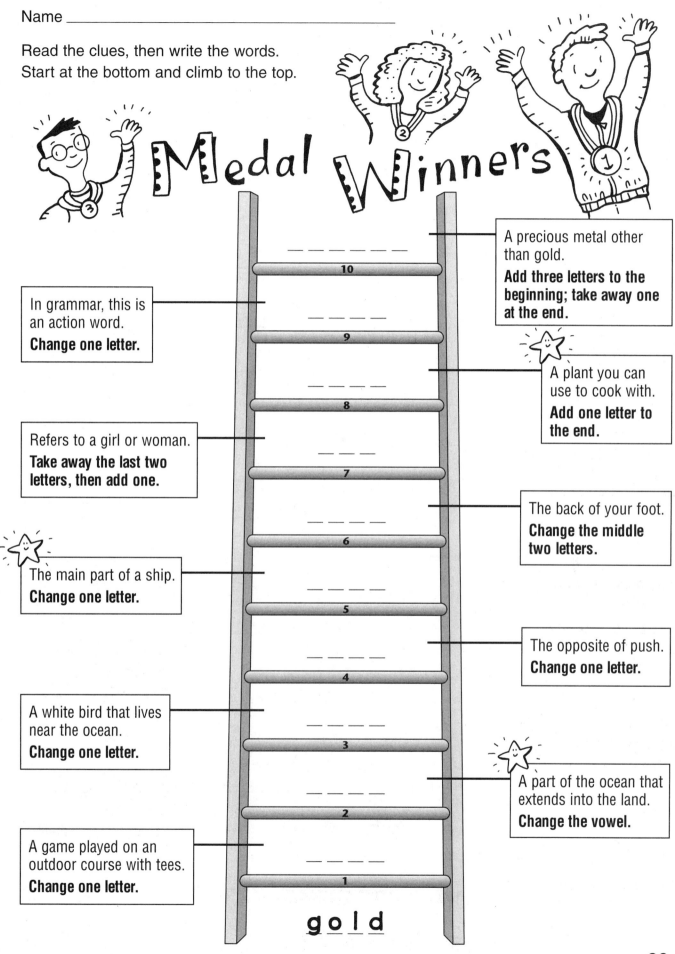

Medal Winners

A precious metal other than gold.
Add three letters to the beginning; take away one at the end.

In grammar, this is an action word.
Change one letter.

A plant you can use to cook with.
Add one letter to the end.

Refers to a girl or woman.
Take away the last two letters, then add one.

The back of your foot.
Change the middle two letters.

The main part of a ship.
Change one letter.

The opposite of push.
Change one letter.

A white bird that lives near the ocean.
Change one letter.

A part of the ocean that extends into the land.
Change the vowel.

A game played on an outdoor course with tees.
Change one letter.

10
9
8
7
6
5
4
3
2
1

g o l d

Interactive Whiteboard Activities: Daily Word Ladders Grades 4–6 © 2012 Timothy V. Rasinski, Scholastic Teaching Resources

Name _____

Read the clues, then write the words.
Start at the bottom and climb to the top.

Fading Light

Absence of light.
Change one letter.

_ _ _ _ _
9

_ _ _ _ _
8

Green space used
for recreation.
Change one letter.

To put objects into a
box, bag, or case.
Change one letter.

_ _ _ _
7

_ _ _ _
6

A large bag made of
coarse cloth.
Change one letter.

Unwell or ill.
**Change the last
two letters.**

_ _ _ _
5

_ _ _ _
4

A written public notice
that gives information
or advertises.
Change the last letter.

To breathe out deeply.
Take away one letter.

_ _ _ _
3

_ _ _ _ _
2

The sense used
for seeing.
Change one letter.

Opposite of left.
Change one letter.

_ _ _ _ _
1

l i g h t

94

Interactive Whiteboard Activities: Daily Word Ladders Grades 4–6 © 2012 Timothy V. Rasinski, Scholastic Teaching Resources

Name _____

Read the clues, then write the words.
Start at the bottom and climb to the top.

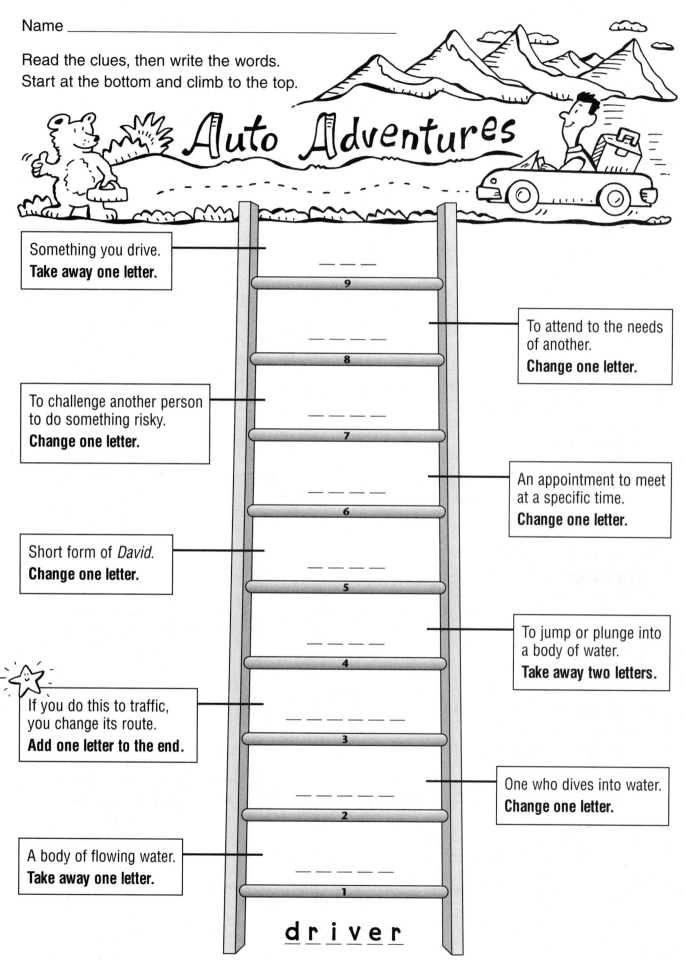

Auto Adventures

Something you drive.
Take away one letter.

_ _ _ _ (9)

To attend to the needs of another.
Change one letter.

_ _ _ _ _ (8)

To challenge another person to do something risky.
Change one letter.

_ _ _ _ (7)

An appointment to meet at a specific time.
Change one letter.

_ _ _ _ _ (6)

Short form of *David*.
Change one letter.

_ _ _ _ (5)

To jump or plunge into a body of water.
Take away two letters.

_ _ _ _ (4)

If you do this to traffic, you change its route.
Add one letter to the end.

_ _ _ _ _ _ (3)

One who dives into water.
Change one letter.

_ _ _ _ _ (2)

A body of flowing water.
Take away one letter.

_ _ _ _ _ (1)

d r i v e r

Name _____

Read the clues, then write the words.
Start at the bottom and climb to the top.

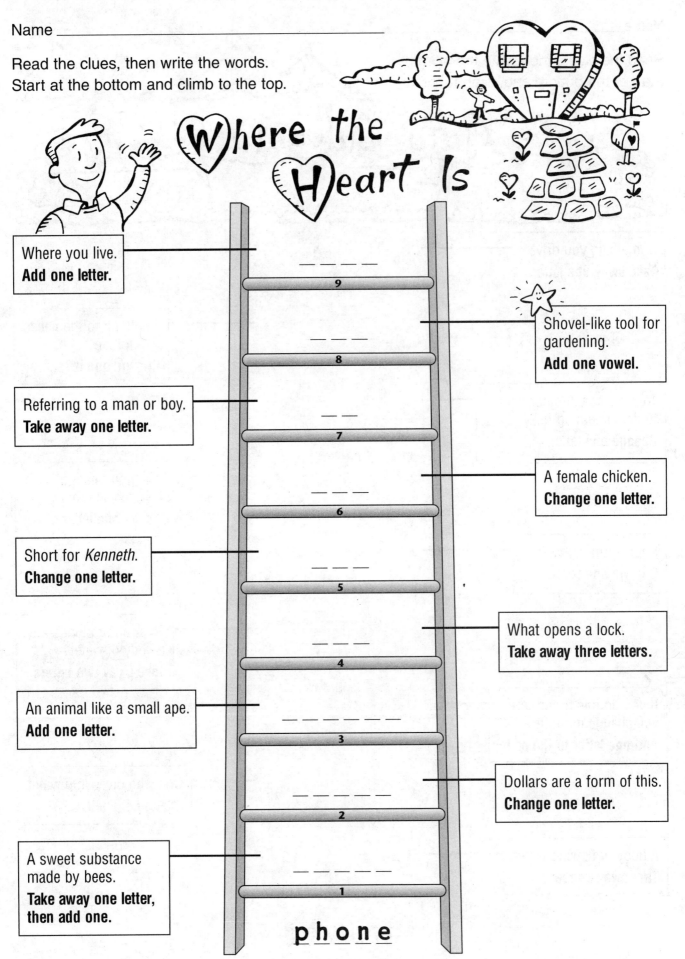

Where the Heart Is

Where you live.
Add one letter.

Shovel-like tool for gardening.
Add one vowel.

Referring to a man or boy.
Take away one letter.

A female chicken.
Change one letter.

Short for *Kenneth*.
Change one letter.

What opens a lock.
Take away three letters.

An animal like a small ape.
Add one letter.

Dollars are a form of this.
Change one letter.

A sweet substance made by bees.
Take away one letter, then add one.

phone

Interactive Whiteboard Activities: Daily Word Ladders Grades 4–6 © 2012 Timothy V. Rasinski, Scholastic Teaching Resources

Name _____

Read the clues, then write the words.
Start at the bottom and climb to the top.

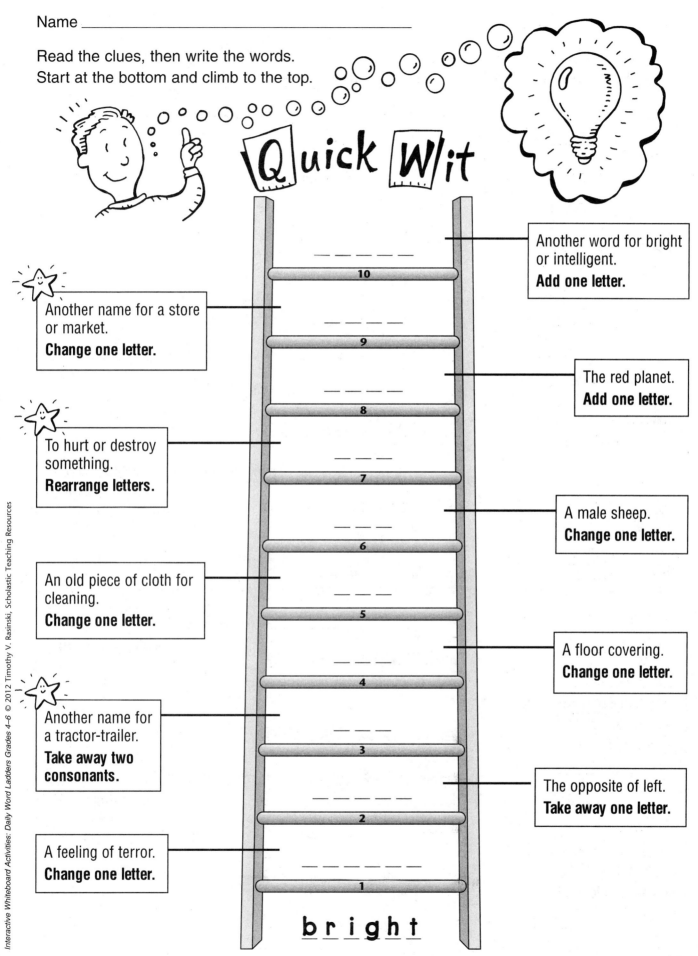

Quick Wit

Another word for bright
or intelligent.
Add one letter.

10 _ _ _ _ _ _

Another name for a store
or market.
Change one letter.

9 _ _ _ _ _

The red planet.
Add one letter.

8 _ _ _ _ _

To hurt or destroy
something.
Rearrange letters.

7 _ _ _ _

A male sheep.
Change one letter.

6 _ _ _ _

An old piece of cloth for
cleaning.
Change one letter.

5 _ _ _ _

A floor covering.
Change one letter.

4 _ _ _ _

Another name for
a tractor-trailer.
**Take away two
consonants.**

3 _ _ _ _

The opposite of left.
Take away one letter.

2 _ _ _ _ _ _

A feeling of terror.
Change one letter.

1 _ _ _ _ _ _

b r i g h t

Name _____

Read the clues, then write the words.
Start at the bottom and climb to the top.

My Family

Another name for a father.
Change one letter.

9 _ _ _

To apply something lightly.
Change the first letter.

8 _ _ _

A short, quick poke.
Change the first letter.

7 _ _ _

Short for *laboratory*.
Change one letter.

6 _ _ _

Another word for *taxi*.
Change one letter.

5 _ _ _

A young bear.
Change one letter.

4 _ _ _

The middle of an ear of corn.
Change one letter.

3 _ _ _

To cry.
Change one letter.

2 _ _ _

An unruly or disorderly group of people.
Change one letter.

1 _ _ _

m o m

Interactive Whiteboard Activities: Daily Word Ladders Grades 4–6 © 2012 Timothy V. Rasinski, Scholastic Teaching Resources

Name _____

Read the clues, then write the words.
Start at the bottom and climb to the top.

Family Ties

Opposite of mother.
Change one letter.

A person who bathes
or goes into water.
Add two letters.

Where you bathe.
Change one letter.

Short for *mathematics*.
Change one letter.

A flying insect that is
attracted to light.
Change one letter.

Referring to two of
something.
Take away one letter.

The liquid part of soup.
Take away two letters.

Opposite of sister.
Add one letter.

To annoy or pester someone.
Add one letter.

An additional or different one.
Take away one letter.

10

9

8

7

6

5

4

3

2

1

m o t h e r

Name _____

Read the clues, then write the words.
Start at the bottom and climb to the top.

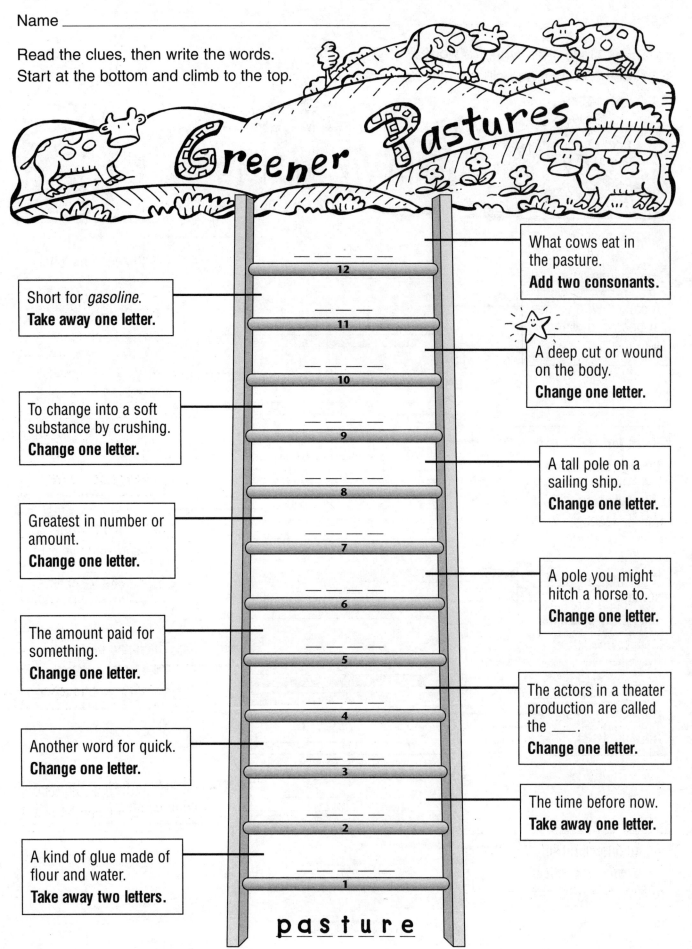

Greener Pastures

What cows eat in the pasture.
Add two consonants.

Short for *gasoline*.
Take away one letter.

A deep cut or wound on the body.
Change one letter.

To change into a soft substance by crushing.
Change one letter.

A tall pole on a sailing ship.
Change one letter.

Greatest in number or amount.
Change one letter.

A pole you might hitch a horse to.
Change one letter.

The amount paid for something.
Change one letter.

The actors in a theater production are called the ____.
Change one letter.

Another word for quick.
Change one letter.

The time before now.
Take away one letter.

A kind of glue made of flour and water.
Take away two letters.

12
11
10
9
8
7
6
5
4
3
2
1

p a s t u r e

Interactive Whiteboard Activities: Daily Word Ladders Grades 4–6 © 2012 Timothy V. Rasinski, Scholastic Teaching Resources

Name _____

Read the clues, then write the words.
Start at the bottom and climb to the top.

Fur Facts

What is missing from someone who is bald.
Change one letter. — 11

Small balls of ice that fall from the sky.
Change one letter. — 10

A corridor or passageway in a building.
Take away one letter. — 9

Shows an action that will take place in the future. "I ___ go."
Change one letter. — 8

The hard covering around some animals.
Add one letter. — 7

To exchange something for money.
Change one letter. — 6

Use this to make a ringing noise.
Change one letter. — 5

A male cow.
Change one letter. — 4

Completely filled.
Change one letter. — 3

To drop or descend.
Change one letter. — 2

A round object used for games.
Change one letter. — 1

b a l d

Name _____

Read the clues, then write the words.
Start at the bottom and climb to the top.

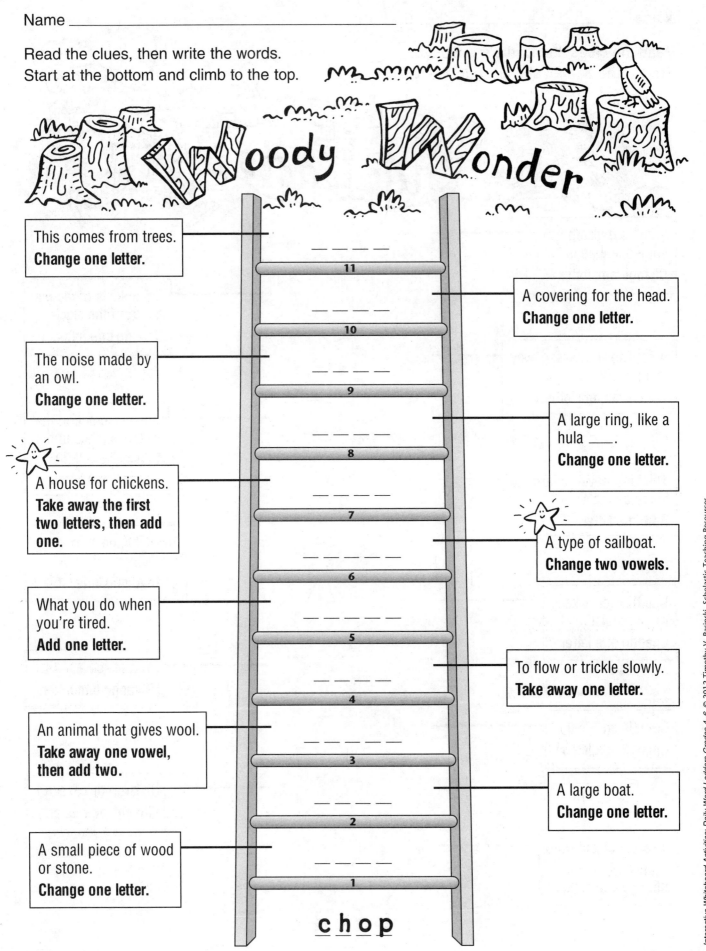

Woody Wonder

This comes from trees.
Change one letter.

11 _ _ _ _

A covering for the head.
Change one letter.

10 _ _ _ _

The noise made by an owl.
Change one letter.

9 _ _ _ _

A large ring, like a hula ___.
Change one letter.

8 _ _ _ _

A house for chickens.
Take away the first two letters, then add one.

7 _ _ _ _

A type of sailboat.
Change two vowels.

6 _ _ _ _ _

What you do when you're tired.
Add one letter.

5 _ _ _ _ _

To flow or trickle slowly.
Take away one letter.

4 _ _ _ _

An animal that gives wool.
Take away one vowel, then add two.

3 _ _ _ _ _

A large boat.
Change one letter.

2 _ _ _ _ _

A small piece of wood or stone.
Change one letter.

1 _ _ _ _

c h o p

Interactive Whiteboard Activities: Daily Word Ladders Grades 4–6 © 2012 Timothy V. Rasinski, Scholastic Teaching Resources

Name _____

Read the clues, then write the words.
Start at the bottom and climb to the top.

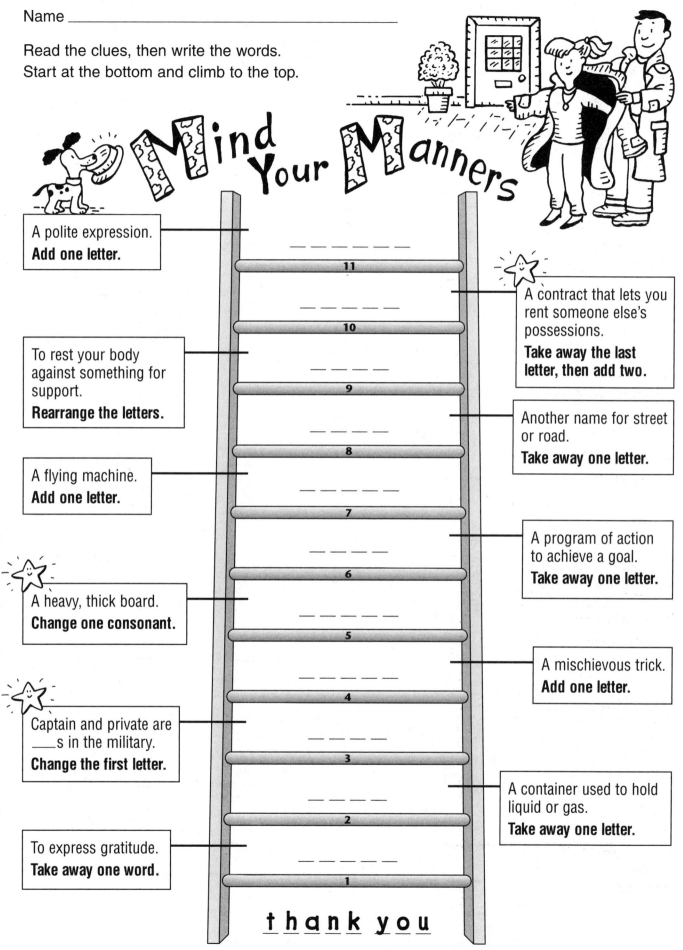

Mind Your Manners

A polite expression.
Add one letter.

— — — — — — — 11

— — — — — 10

A contract that lets you rent someone else's possessions.
Take away the last letter, then add two.

To rest your body against something for support.
Rearrange the letters.

— — — — — 9

— — — — 8

Another name for street or road.
Take away one letter.

A flying machine.
Add one letter.

— — — — — 7

A program of action to achieve a goal.
Take away one letter.

— — — — 6

A heavy, thick board.
Change one consonant.

— — — — — 5

A mischievous trick.
Add one letter.

— — — — — 4

Captain and private are ___ s in the military.
Change the first letter.

— — — — 3

A container used to hold liquid or gas.
Take away one letter.

— — — — 2

To express gratitude.
Take away one word.

— — — — — 1

t h a n k   y o u

Name _____

Read the clues, then write the words.
Start at the bottom and climb to the top.

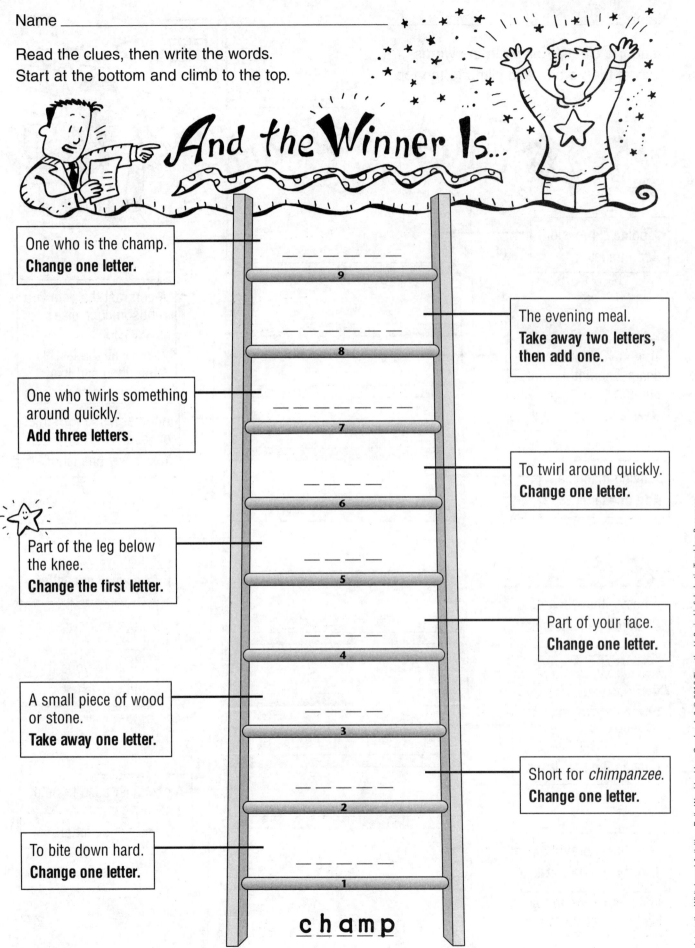

And the Winner Is...

One who is the champ.
Change one letter.

The evening meal.
Take away two letters, then add one.

One who twirls something around quickly.
Add three letters.

To twirl around quickly.
Change one letter.

Part of the leg below the knee.
Change the first letter.

Part of your face.
Change one letter.

A small piece of wood or stone.
Take away one letter.

Short for *chimpanzee*.
Change one letter.

To bite down hard.
Change one letter.

9 _____

8 _____

7 _____

6 ____

5 ____

4 ____

3 ____

2 _____

1 _____

c h a m p

Interactive Whiteboard Activities: Daily Word Ladders Grades 4–6 © 2012 Timothy V. Rasinski, Scholastic Teaching Resources

Name _____

Read the clues, then write the words.
Start at the bottom and climb to the top.

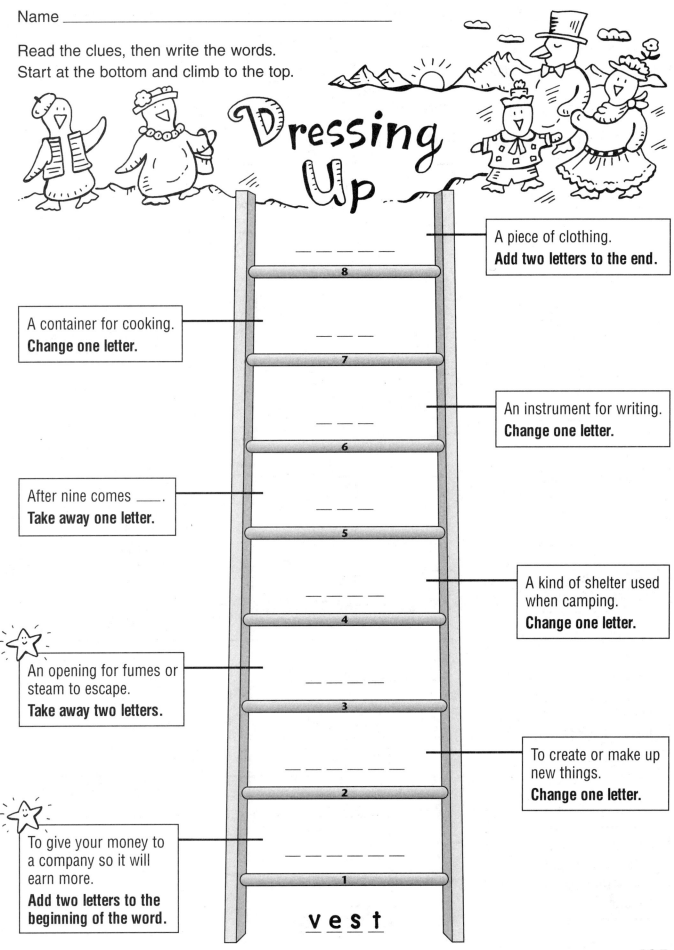

Dressing Up

A piece of clothing.
Add two letters to the end.

8 _ _ _ _ _ _

A container for cooking.
Change one letter.

7 _ _ _ _

An instrument for writing.
Change one letter.

6 _ _ _ _

After nine comes ____.
Take away one letter.

5 _ _ _

A kind of shelter used
when camping.
Change one letter.

4 _ _ _ _

An opening for fumes or
steam to escape.
Take away two letters.

3 _ _ _ _

To create or make up
new things.
Change one letter.

2 _ _ _ _ _

To give your money to
a company so it will
earn more.
**Add two letters to the
beginning of the word.**

1 _ _ _ _ _

v e s t

Name _____

Read the clues, then write the words.
Start at the bottom and climb to the top.

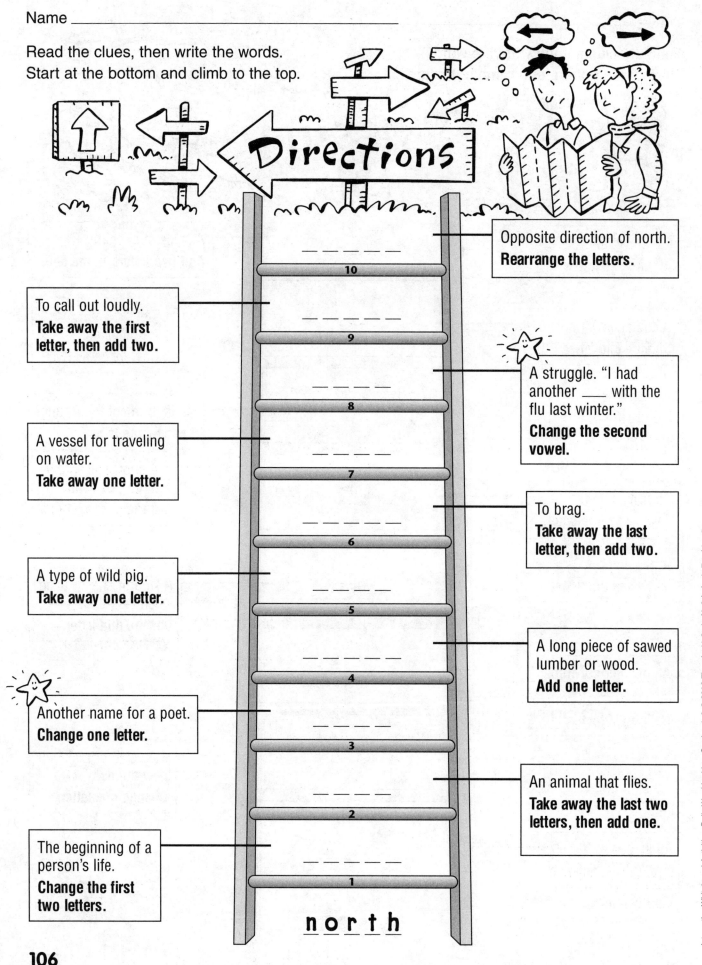

Directions

Opposite direction of north.
Rearrange the letters.

To call out loudly.
Take away the first letter, then add two.

A struggle. "I had another ___ with the flu last winter."
Change the second vowel.

A vessel for traveling on water.
Take away one letter.

To brag.
Take away the last letter, then add two.

A type of wild pig.
Take away one letter.

A long piece of sawed lumber or wood.
Add one letter.

Another name for a poet.
Change one letter.

An animal that flies.
Take away the last two letters, then add one.

The beginning of a person's life.
Change the first two letters.

n o r t h

Interactive Whiteboard Activities: Daily Word Ladders Grades 4–6 © 2012 Timothy V. Rasinski, Scholastic Teaching Resources

Name _____

Read the clues, then write the words.
Start at the bottom and climb to the top.

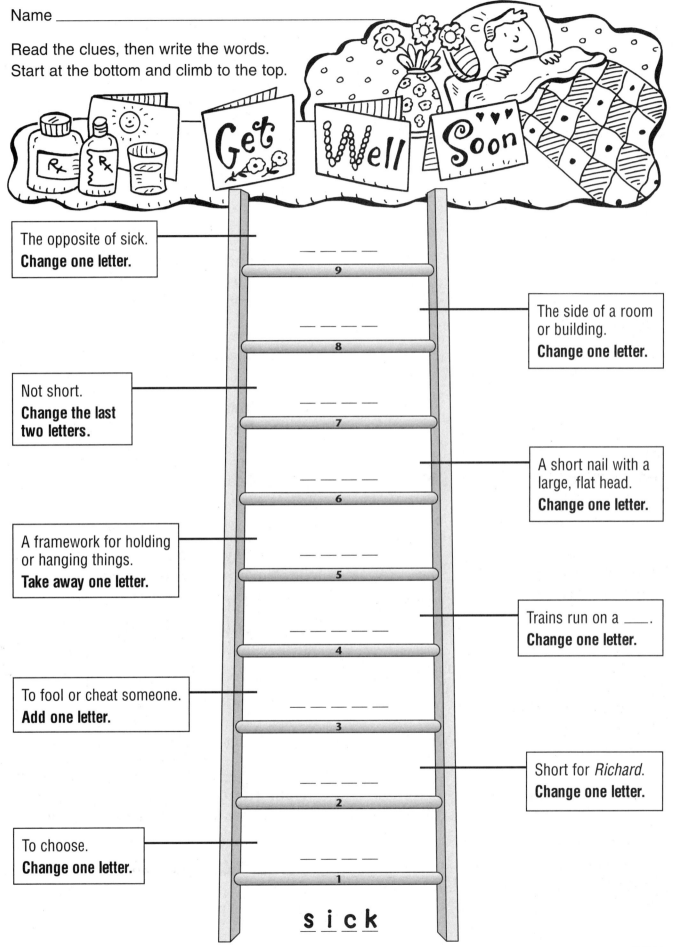

The opposite of sick.
Change one letter.

9 _ _ _ _ _

The side of a room or building.
Change one letter.

8 _ _ _ _

Not short.
Change the last two letters.

7 _ _ _ _

A short nail with a large, flat head.
Change one letter.

6 _ _ _ _

A framework for holding or hanging things.
Take away one letter.

5 _ _ _ _

Trains run on a ___.
Change one letter.

4 _ _ _ _

To fool or cheat someone.
Add one letter.

3 _ _ _ _

Short for *Richard*.
Change one letter.

2 _ _ _ _

To choose.
Change one letter.

1 _ _ _ _

s i c k

Answer Key

Eat Your Vegetables, page 7
vegetable, table, stable, stab, slab, slob, slosh, slash, dash, dish, radish

Money Matters, page 8
nickel, pickle, pick, pink, stink, sting, sing, sang, sane, same, dame, dime

Outerwear, page 9
sweater, sweat, sweet, sweeten, ten, ton, stone, notes, not, jot, jock, Jack, jacket

Behind the Wheel, page 10
car, scar, scare, share, sharp, harp, hare, dare, Dave, dive, diver, driver

Give a Little, page 11
give, live, liver, diver, dive, hive, have, shave, shake, snake, stake, take

Things That Go Bump in the Night, page 12
vampire, expire, retire, tire, fire, fine, tine, tone, ton, ten, net, bet, bat

Toothsome, page 13
tooth, toot, soot, soon, son, Don, don't, dent, dentist

Say Cheese, page 14
picture, capture, cap, cape, escape, estate, state, taste, haste, hate, hat, hot, photo

Hat Head, page 15
hat, hate, haste, waste, aster, asterisk, risk, disk, duck, luck, lack, lap, cap

In the Money, page 16
million, billion, lion, stallion, stall, still, till, tall, toll, doll, dollar

Meet and Greet, page 17
convention, invention, intention, tension, pension, suspension, suspense, suspend, spend, speed, seed, meet, meeting

Cool Drinks, page 18
ice, Alice, malice, chalice, chalk, stalk, talk, walk, walker, water

Stars and Stripes, page 19
country, county, count, aunt, tuna, tundra, drain, rain, rail, nail, nation

In My Room, page 20
bed, bled, red, read, bread, break, brook, brood, broom, boom, room

Sleepytime, page 21
pillow, pill, fill, fall, tall, talk, tank, bank, blank, blanket

Giving Thanks, page 22
grateful, grate, gate, gateway, getaway, away, awful, thankful

Express Mail, page 23
deliver, liver, live, line, lime, slime, slim, slam, Sam, sad, sand, send

Stormy Days, page 24
rain, ran, raw, war, wore, swore, sword, words, word, lord, loud, cloud

Official Officers, page 25
private, pirate, irate, rate, grate, generate, generation, generally, general

Bucket Brigade, page 26
bucket, buck, duck, duct, conduct, conductor, doctor, dock, mock, Mick, pick, pack, pail

Sweet Things, page 27
caramel, camel, came, cane, sane, same, seam, seat, sweat, sweet

Here to There, page 28
march, Mars, mare, more, wore, were, where, here, hire, hare, ware, wart, walk

Good Eating, page 29
digest, diet, die, dim, dam, mad, made, mat, eat

That's Entertainment, page 30
television, vision, visit, sit, set, seat, heat, hat, rat, ratio, radio

All Is Forgiven, page 31
forgive, give, live, liver, liter, later, lather, gather, together, get, forget

Go, Go, Go, page 32
automobile, mobile, mob, cob, cot, Scot, scat, scab, cab, car

All in the Family, page 33
uncle, unclear, nuclear, clear, learn, earn, earnest, ear, are, art, ant, aunt

Give a Dog a Bone, page 34
dog, dig, din, ding, ring, wring, bring, big, bag, bang, bong, bone

Dinner's Ready, page 35
vegetable, table, cable, cab, baby, ban, fan, fat, fate, mate, meat

Happy Birthday, page 36
birthday, birth, both, bath, wrath, wreath, wreck, rock, rack, rake, cake

Chew on This, page 37
bite, bit, but, hut, shut, shot, shop, hop, chop, chow, chew

Peaks and Valleys, page 38
high, sigh, sight, right, rig, rag, raw, saw, law, low

A Rose Is a Rose, page 39
flower, lower, low, slow, slot, lot, not, knot, note, nose, rose

Childhood, page 40
child, mild, mind, wind, win, pin, spin, span, pan, pad, dad, did, kid

Cheese Eaters, page 41
mouse, house, hose, chose, chase, base, bash, bath, bat, rat

Frosty Fun, page 42
snow, now, not, dot, dog, dig, ding, king, kin, win, winter

Seaworthy, page 43
ocean, bean, bead, beard, heard, heart, heat, seat, seal, sea

Sew Sew, page 44
sew, sell, sill, still, skill, kill, kilt, wilt, wit, witch, itch, stitch

Save Your Pennies, page 45
penny, pen, nope, open, spend, speed, seed, send, sent, cent

Right or Wrong, page 46
true, blue, clue, club, cub, hub, hum, ham, hall, fall, false

Precipitation Puzzle, page 47
rain, chain, chin, shin, shine, shingle, single, sing, wing, whip, wrap, crop, drop

Snow Day, page 48
blizzard, lizard, liar, rail, rain, grain, grin, grow, row, now, snow

Winter Wear, page 49
coat, coal, coil, oil, lion, stallion, talon, alone, lone, love, gloves

Out of This World, page 50
Venus, vent, sent, spent, pen, men, man, can, car, mar, Mars

Fried Snacks, page 51
french, trench, wrench, wren, renew, newer, fewer, fee, free, fry

Candlelight, page 52
candle, handle, hand, hard, shard, share, hare, fare, flare, flame

Car Trouble, page 53
flat, inflate, late, slate, tales, tiles, tile, time, tide, tire

Play Date, page 54
play, plan, plane, plates, staple, stable, able, amble, ramble, rumble, humble, hum, chum

Beautiful Day, page 55
blue, clue, glue, glee, flee, flea, flew, fly, sly, sky

Ruling the Roost, page 56
rooster, roost, roast, toast, coast, cast, cat, hat, hit, chick, chicken

New and Not-So-New, page 57
new, few, dew, sew, sow, now, how, show, shown, own, owl, old

Midday Meal, page 58
lunch, launch, laundry, dry, day, say, sap, sip, sipper, supper

Growing Up, page 59
short, shore, shoe, show, slow, plow, blow, below, belong, long

Wedding Words, page 60
bride, stride, ride, rid, rod, rode, road, roam, room, groom

Friendship, page 61
friend, end, send, sent, set, bet, but, cut, cute, chute, chum

Rub-a-Dub-Dub, page 62
scrub, rub, rib, crib, cob, rob, throb, broth, both, bath

Underwater, page 63
dive, dime, chime, chimp, champ, ham, hum, hub, cub, Cuba, scuba

Hear This, page 64
scream, cream, cram, cramp, ramp, ram, rat, rot, trot, trout, shout

Brainy Bird, page 65
eagle, beagle, bagel, bugle, bungle, bundle, candle, handle, hand, Hank, hack, hawk

Itchy and Scratchy, page 66
itch, inch, pinch, punch, lunch, hunch, hutch, hitch, pitch, patch, catch, scratch

Drinking Vessels, page 67
glass, lass, last, least, yeast, year, bear, beep, jeep, jump, slump, pump, cup

Good Books, page 68
story, store, ore, chore, core, bore, bone, boo, book

Land of the Free, page 69
liberty, tribe, bride, pride, ride, rid, red, read, reed, freed, freedom

Corny!, page 70
maize, maze, made, jade, jab, job, cob, con, coin, corn

School Days, page 71
school, cool, coal, cola, cold, scold, sold, hold, hole, home

Jobs for Grownups, page 72
teacher, teach, each, ache, acre, care, pare, parent

Ship Shape, page 73
navy, naval, novel, shovel, shove, shave, shape, share, shame, ham, him, hip, ship

Suppertime, page 74
supper, super, sugar, rag, drag, drug, dug, dig, din, diner, dinner

Just a Spoonful, page 75
sweet, sweat, seat, heat, hut, gut, tug, chug, hug, rug, shrug, sugar

Flower Power, page 76
petal, pedal, penal, panel, pane, pave, shave, shove, show, how, low, flow, flower

24 Hours, page 77
night, might, right, bright, big, jig, jag, jay, day

Horse Sense, page 78
colt, cost, host, most, mast, mart, mare, more, Morse, horse

Voting Booth, page 79
ballot, ball, ballet, let, lot, tot, tote, note, vote

Sailing, page 80
sail, snail, ail, aim, claim, clam, calm, palm, pal, pat, cat, coat, boat

Bunny Tales, page 81
rabbit, bit, bat, fat, far, car, scar, scare, care, hare

Good Hare Day, page 82
hare, share, sharp, harp, carp, card, bard, bare, bar, bat, but, bun, bunny

Very Fishy, page 83
minnow, window, wind, win, wine, whine, shine, shrine, shrimp

Beasts of Burden, page 84
horse, shore, chore, core, more, mere, mare, care, came, camel

Apple for Teacher, page 85
faculty, faulty, fault, felt, fell, tell, tall, tam, team, teach

Art Smart, page 86
art, part, park, pack, tack, talk, tall, mall, all, alley, galley, gallery

Uphill, page 87
mountain, mount, mound, found, hound, hind, hint, hunt, hull, hill

Globe Guessing, page 88
south, mouth, out, shout, pout, pot, port, pore, pole

Fish Wish, page 89
sturgeon, surgeon, surge, splurge, purge, purse, pure, cure, core, fire, fir, fit, fish

From the Ground Up, page 90
reconstruct, construct, instruct, destruct, distract, distrust, trust, brush, bush, bud, build, rebuild

Strength Training, page 91
weak, week, weed, reed, read, road, roach, coach, couch, touch, tough

Getting the Message, page 92
message, massage, mass, miss, mist, wrist, west, nest, net, not, note

Medal Winners, page 93
gold, golf, gulf, gull, pull, hull, heel, her, herb, verb, silver

Fading Light, page 94
light, right, sight, sigh, sign, sick, sack, pack, park, dark